MIND OVER MATTER

MIND OVER MATTER

Reflections
on Buddhism
in the West

Tarthang Tulku

Dharma Publishing

Illustrations
Cover: The Odiyan Mandala
Page 1: Guru Padmasambhava
Page 183: Vajrākṣobhya Mandala

Library of Congress Control Number: 2001095842
ISBN: 0–89800–322–9

Printed in the USA by Dharma Press

10 9 8 7 6 5 4 3 2 1

To all students of the Dharma
May your efforts be blessed with success

Contents

Part One
REFLECTIONS ON BUDDHISM IN THE WEST

Part Two
CONVERSATIONS WITH TARTHANG TULKU

Introduction

*T*he essays published in this book were initially prepared for *Annals of the Tibetan Nyingma Meditation Center, Volume Five,* an ongoing history and archival record of the activities of the organizations under my direction. I wrote them in order to share with members of our community my thoughts on how Buddhism is entering the West. It was my hope that these observations, based on nearly thirty years of living and working in America, would help my students identify topics important to the future of the Dharma and encourage them to look more closely at attitudes and patterns that tend to cloud their understanding. I wished also to point out the value of the work they are doing and emphasize how effectively this work can lay the foundation for a genuine transmission of the Buddhist teachings.

After this fifth volume of the *Annals* was published in 1997, many of our members and friends commented on the importance of the topics covered in these essays and asked if these writings could be made available to the general public. The editors of Dharma Publishing volunteered to shape them into a book, and members of our centers in Brazil,

Germany, and Holland asked for permission to translate and publish the resulting work. The interviews at the end of the book were compiled from the *Annals* and other sources.

It is my hope that these reflections will be useful to everyone interested in future of the Dharma in the West. While the stream that is carrying the Dharma to the West may flow more quietly than other currents of change demanding our attention, transmission of the Dharma is among the most important events of our era. In our uncertain times, the teachings of the Buddha offer fresh perspectives and knowledge that can stabilize the mind. They hold forth the possibility of transformation at the deepest level of our being. Will the Dharma take hold deeply enough for a genuine transmission to take place? Or will Western students accept only some aspects of the Dharma, failing to comprehend how all the elements of the tradition work together to support a more enlightened understanding?

Like so many others who have come to America over the past two centuries, I have attempted to share the heritage of my native land with the people of this country. In my own way, I have lived out the American dream, discovering in this new land the openness and tolerance that have allowed me to work for the values that I hold most dear. This is the promise of America, the vision that uplifts and inspires, and I cannot express strongly enought my thanks that this promise can still be fulfilled.

In memory of my teachers, for the sake of the Tibetan people, and for the benefit of the Dharma, I am profoundly grateful to have been given this opportunity to create a home for the Dharma in the West and accomplish projects that help preserve and transmit the teachings of my tradition. The results we have achieved are my gestures of thanks for the freedoms America offers and for the kindness I have been shown here. The welcoming openness of this land evokes the blessings of Padmasambhava, the master who revealed the depths of the Buddha's teachings for the welfare of beings everywhere. Whatever I have done has been possible only because of these blessings and the support I have received from my parents and relatives, my people, my Dharma friends and students, and most especially my holy masters.

May the power of the teachings and the wisdom of the Enlightened Lineage manifest for the people of this land and this age, and also throughout all of space and time. May the sun of the Dharma continue to shine brightly, bringing to maturity the mandala garden where realization unfolds spontaneously. May the flowers of achievement blossom and the symbols of the Dharma bear rich fruit. May the path always remain available for all who wish to embark on it, and may the universe itself become a mandala of realization.

PART ONE

Reflections on Buddhism in the West

*When the iron bird flies
and horses run on wheels,
the Tibetan people will be scattered like ants
across the face of the world,
and the Dharma will come
to the land of the red-faced men.*

—Padmasambhava

Questions of Transmission

*T*hrough rare good fortune, I was born in a home and a land where the teachings of the Buddha were honored and practiced. The influence of my family and my early years at Tarthang monastery taught me to appreciate the difference between a life shaped by samsaric concerns and one devoted to the goal of freeing all beings from suffering.

As I grew older, I had the opportunity to meet and study with some of the greatest masters of this century, and to see in their person the Dharma in action. Though my studies and practice were limited in scope, I received a basic foundation in the teachings of the Three Yānas, including the traditions of the Sūtras and the śāstras, the Mantrayāna, and the special teachings of the Nyingma school. Most important, the bountiful blessings and generous counsel bestowed upon me by my teachers taught me to shape my life toward the Dharma, the source of all good.

The guidance and blessings I received as a youth inspired me to work wholeheartedly for the Dharma, dedicating whatever merit my actions accumulated to the welfare of others and sharing to the best of my ability the understanding I had been able to attain. Although I can never hope to repay the great kindness shown to me by my teachers, I have sought through my actions to commemorate their blessings and pass on their good works, fulfilling their wishes to the best of my ability. Since leaving Tibet almost forty years ago, I have continually directed my energy toward projects that I believed could serve the Dharma and bring some small measure of benefit to others.

For the past thirty years I have carried out this work primarily in the West. During this time, the circumstances of my daily work have been my teacher. Through facing the challenges that arise whenever anyone seeks to accomplish something of value, I have experienced directly the truth of many of the teachings that I studied as a boy and as a young man. Although I did not pursue the more formal style of practice that I would have undertaken had Tibetan civilization not been disrupted, the insights I have received through my work in the world have steadily deepened my appreciation for the lineage of enlightened realization. Today my dedication to sharing with others the truth and value of the Dharma is as strong as ever.

The decades I have spent in the West, together with the work I have done, have given me a broader perspective on the changes that traditional

Buddhism is undergoing, both among the Tibetan people and here in the West. I have sought in these pages to share some of this perspective. These reflections may be of interest not only to those who have worked with me, but also to others who are actively engaged in the transmission of the Dharma in these rapidly evolving times, or simply curious about the historic meeting of Buddhism with the modern world.

One issue that has concerned me in recent years is the prospect for fruitful and meaningful interaction between traditional Tibetan Dharma teachers and the small but growing number of Buddhists in lands new to the Dharma. While each Dharma center and each teacher is different, certain general tendencies come into play in such interactions, and I have had the opportunity to observe many of them first hand and in detail in our own centers. I am especially interested in identifying and commenting on some of these trends, for to be aware of such patterns from the outset is like having a blueprint before beginning to build a house: It can help avoid mistakes and false starts that lead to difficulties later on. Although it may not always be evident on the surface, many of the reflections I present here are inspired by this intention.

The growth of the Dharma as it makes its way in the modern world has been unstructured, even chaotic. Given the present historical circumstances, this is to be expected, but it may still result in confusion about Buddhism and the essentials of its practice. Today some Dharma teachers emphasize meditation while others focus on scholarship, and still others give preeminence to ritual or blessings and initiations. While all of these approaches are valid, their variety underscores the importance of developing and transmitting a comprehensive understanding that integrates all these aspects. Without informed appreciation for the vast scope of the teachings, their application, and how they cohere, Dharma students may begin to believe that there are contradictions or conflicts in the teachings, where in fact none exist.

In these fragmented times, there is a real danger that Buddhism too may come to be understood in various fragmentary forms. Some will label it as a sophisticated philosophical system, others as a set of practices with therapeutic power, still others as a system of ethical injunctions that link peace and fellowship with the cultivation of inner serenity. For others, it will be seen primarily as a form of devotional religion, or as complex rituals for invoking various powers and deities. But ultimately none of these aspects can stand on its own. It is essential to understand the whole range of the Dharma: its historical development, its contributions to every field of human knowledge, and the vast range of its teachings and practices. Only when students and practitioners of Buddhism operate from this foundation can they learn to comprehend the purpose of the Dharma and pass on its full significance to others.

In particular, I am concerned that in the future students new to the Dharma have the opportunity— and accept the responsibility—to engage the traditions of Tibetan Buddhism with an open mind. Although we live in a time and place very different from the Tibet I knew as a youth, this does not mean that the traditional forms of the teachings can simply be discarded. Eventually new ways of approaching the Dharma, with qualities appropriate to the modern world, may develop. For now, however, it is too soon to turn away from the wisdom embodied in the teachings and forms of practice passed down by the enlightened masters of the past. If new students attempt to take hold of the Dharma too quickly, if they shape the Dharma in light of their own understanding before genuine realization has emerged, and if they use it to serve their own purposes, there is a very real danger that the full power and wisdom of the Dharma will be drained away.

The reflections I present here address such issues from a variety of perspectives. The thoughts they express have taken shape in the course of numerous discussions with friends and students, and I have attempted to deal with the questions I am most frequently asked and the concerns I most often hear expressed. I do not expect every reader to agree with all that I have to say, but I sincerely hope that even those who disagree with me will benefit from thinking through these issues carefully.

Tibetan Buddhism
in the World Today

*A*lmost forty years have passed since the
Communist takeover in Tibet and the resulting Tibetan diaspora. Accurately predicted
by Padmasambhava twelve centuries ago, these cat-
astrophic events have exposed Tibetan culture and
the Tibetans themselves to pressures that few people in history have ever successfully withstood. The
effects have been momentous: in Tibet, among the
refugee communities, and for the Dharma throughout the world.

The Dharma in Present-day Tibet

I have visited Tibet several times in recent years,
and I find that the consequences of the systematic
campaign of cultural disruption instituted under
Chinese rule are visible everywhere. For more than
twenty years—an entire generation—it was virtually
impossible to practice the Dharma in the Land of
Snow. Now some degree of Buddhist training and
practice is once again permitted, but the damage
has been done. A few in the new generation may be
eager to restore the traditions of their homeland,

but when their understanding of what has been lost is fragmentary, how can they even begin?

The occupying forces did more than destroy temples, monasteries, and libraries by the thousands. As the world well knows, they made it their aim to have the Tibetans accept Chinese values and culture as filtered through the ideology of Communism. In this they were largely successful. Although the people of Tibet continue to think of themselves as Buddhists, they have been systematically 're-educated' or reprogrammed to reject the values that guided Tibetan culture for a thousand years. The Chinese have taught generations of Tibetan children to believe that their heritage was corrupt and deserved to be swept away. Very likely they were sincere in propagating this view, for their training blinded them to the benefits that Tibetan society conferred upon its people.

Shaped by their own cultural conditioning, the Chinese have treated the Tibetan people like backward savages unworthy of respect. They have destroyed Tibetan civilization and its artifacts, exploited Tibet's natural resources, put great lamas to death, and exercised complete control over the education of children and the activities of the population at large. No matter what their motivation, what they have done to my people and my land is something I do not believe can ever be justified.

My impression from my own travels, confirmed by conversations with lamas and ordinary people who lived through this whole dark era, is that the treatment inflicted on Tibet by the Han Chinese has taken a tremendous toll. Today most Tibetans struggle to live from day to day. They have no vision of what is spiritually possible for human beings. Young people no longer look to their own tradition for inspiration, and they find it difficult to take seriously the claim that Tibetan culture has great treasures to offer the world. If they do have the energy to look beyond personal concerns, they set their sights on modernizing their country, which they have been taught to regard as poorly equipped to deal with present-day realities.

Even individuals who reject this narrowly materialistic view find it difficult to consider any real alternative. Though they may hope for something better, they see it as coming from outside Tibet: perhaps from the Tibetan government in exile, or from Western countries who support the rights of cultures to determine their own destinies. But today, after forty years of waiting, these hopes too are beginning to fade.

This brief sketch may seem unduly grim. I sincerely hope that I am wrong, and I will certainly continue to support the Dharma in Tibet as fully as I can. Yet a vital way of life is gone forever. In my heart I do not expect that Tibet will ever fully recover from the tragic events of the past decades.

Tibetan Dharma in Exile

When I consider the situation for Tibetans in exile, I can speak more directly from personal experience. Those of us who fled our homeland in the late 1950s and early 1960s arrived in India and Nepal with few possessions, not knowing what the future would hold. India, itself a poor country, was deeply generous in receiving and accommodating us as best she could. We looked upon India with deep respect as the Ārya land where the Buddha was enlightened, and we were deeply grateful for her kindness. Yet very soon we realized that we were on our own.

As we discovered how great was the damage inflicted on our homeland, and our hopes for a speedy return began to dim, we had to confront the enormity and bleakness of our situation. Like most refugees, we had to cope with a new environment, extreme poverty, and the wrenching shock of losing our entire world. But for us, the trauma was even greater, for the world that had disappeared from under our feet was separated from our new surroundings not only by high mountain peaks, but by a vast cultural divide. Those of us who had received the benefit of a classic Tibetan monastic education grieved to think that the cultural treasures and profound teachings we had cherished might well vanish from the face of the earth.

Those first few years were difficult indeed. It is hard to remember today how poorly equipped we were for making our way in the modern world, and how completely unfamiliar we were with the new society in which we found ourselves. Many among us died, victims of diseases that our bodies could not fight off, a climate that shocked our bodies and nervous systems, lack of basic medical care, or a failure to understand the rules of hygiene necessary in this new environment. Others were simply stunned into giving up from the heartbreak of losing friends, family, and culture.

Still, many of us struggled on. We realized that the future of the Tibetan people might well be up to us, and we were determined to find our footing, gain a measure of economic security, and start on the project of renewing our culture. Those of us who were young and vigorous began to hope that we could build the foundation for a new way of life.

When I left India in 1968, the situation of the Tibetan refugees had certainly improved, but in many ways it was still precarious. By the time I returned, however, twenty-one years later, a dramatic transformation had taken place. Tibetan refugee communities today are relatively prosperous, and they have established hundreds of schools, monasteries, and retreat centers where the cultural traditions of the Tibetan people can be preserved and passed on. I see this clearly at the annual Nyingma Monlam Chenmo in Bodh Gayā, where representatives of some three hundred different Nyingma centers attend, most from institutions founded since 1959. Tens of thousands of laypersons have learned the skills that make it possible to survive and do well in the circumstances of contemporary society. Among them are doctors, teachers, administrators, and others who are bringing modern knowledge into the exile community.

The success of the Tibetans in exile has given lamas the resources to do much to preserve their traditions. In each of the four major schools of Tibetan Buddhism, individuals who escaped Tibet as young children have been trained as scholars and practitioners of Dharma, and great efforts have been made to give the new tulkus born in exile a solid education in their own traditions. Tulkus, khenpos, Dharma teachers, yogins, monks, and lay Dharma practitioners are all following the traditional path.

Yet this is only a part of the story. Great as the accomplishments over the past few decades have been, much of what made Tibet unique has been lost forever, beyond the power of even the most skillful and dedicated members of the Tibetan community in exile to recover. As older Tibetans pass away, a whole way of life is going with them. Most Tibetan refugees alive today have never seen Tibet, and many of the rest were too young when they fled their homes to remember the reality of Tibetan civilization. Of those left alive who do remember what Tibet was really like, very few had the benefit of receiving while still in their homeland a comprehensive training in the Dharma, a process that could easily take twenty-five years or longer.

In the Tibet I knew, every monastery and retreat center had its own tradition and discipline. Lamas were able to participate in a way of life wholly devoted to the Dharma, grounded in traditions of practice passed down through the centuries. At each of the great centers of learning and religious practice, scores of individuals dedicated themselves completely to intensive practice and study. Most monasteries were isolated, and monks, nuns, and lay practitioners had little contact with the outside world. Other members of society gave their full faith and devotion to the monastic community, and the wealthy considered it a privilege and a sacred obligation to support the Sangha.

Today that way of life has vanished. The quality of instruction at the new monasteries and shedras (institutes of higher learning) in India and Nepal may well be high, but the traditions that sustained Dharma knowledge have been profoundly transformed by their abrupt encounter with the modern world. In the exile community, most monks and nuns live in close contact with conventional society, with all its distractions and temptations. Among the lay community, individuals are bombarded by media that promote values opposed to the traditions of the Dharma, introducing distractions and creating tensions that were formerly unknown. The old tradition of patronage has almost died out, making it difficult for serious practitioners to devote themselves fully to the teachings. All these developments strain the ties that formerly held Tibetan society together. Such changes affect the quality of practice among the Sangha.

Two Different Ways of Life

The contrast I am pointing out is almost too fundamental to describe. In the old Tibet, lamas and yogins taught each new generation of Dharma practitioners that samsara was the enemy, a dangerous and potentially destructive trap for anyone who wished to follow in the footsteps of the Enlightened Lineage. Religious practice and study were presented as the best path for attaining inner joy, and young lamas and monks grew up learning that real satisfaction came from dedicating one's efforts to the welfare of all beings. Texts written two hundred or even two thousand years earlier still offered the best guidance for living one's life, and success meant pursuing a calling almost identical to one practiced for centuries.

In a world where people lived close to nature, the traditional teaching that all sentient beings had once been one's mother and father took on a natural, self-evident quality. With few distractions and a way of life that allowed ample time for reflection, practice, and contemplation, a vocation centered on religious practice seemed completely appropriate. Particularly in the remote mountain valleys, such as the one where I grew up, the emotional problems that beset the modern world were virtually unknown. Wherever one traveled, one encountered colorful prayer flags flying in the breezes, stupas and other monuments erected at places of power, the inspiring presence of the great monasteries and temples, the retreat huts of solitary yogins, and the sounds of mantra and ceremonies. Dharma practice was a part of nature, imparting its flavor to the land and to all living things. Self-discipline came easily in such a setting, and respect for knowledge and for the lineage grew naturally.

In the larger society that sustained the great monasteries and the hundreds of thousands of dedicated Dharma practitioners of Tibet, respect and admiration for a way of life devoted to the Dharma was universal. Families gladly supported their children or their brothers and sisters as they pursued their studies. Those who became exemplars of the Dharma, dedicating their lives to practice and study for the sake of freeing all beings from the karmic pain and confusion of samsara, were recognized as great cultural heroes.

This interplay of forces had a positive, self-fulfilling effect. Since Dharma practitioners were expected to be good examples, even those whose understanding and practice were limited were compelled to act in wholesome ways. Whatever may have been going on within their hearts, they at least had to pretend to be mindful, compassionate, and knowledgeable, and in this way they fostered the traditional values of caring and devotion, and contributed to the continuity and stability of society and the transmission of the teachings.

In the exile communities, every one of these elements has vanished or been transformed almost beyond recognition. Tibetan exiles live in a world where countless lifestyles and values compete for their attention, and the certainties that once seemed so solid and reliable can no longer be maintained. While schools in the exile community teach Tibetan culture and history, each successive generation grows up with less understanding of the way that the Dharma in Tibet shaped all aspects of life. The new generation of Tibetans born in exile lacks direct contact with the old Tibetan civilization; unlike their parents they do not even have the personal experience of loss that would keep alive a determination to restore what had once been theirs.

Nowadays there are young Tibetans in the refugee communities who accept views not wholly different from those that the Chinese rulers have sought to impose in Tibet itself. Convinced that their own tradition is backward and will not equip them to deal with the modern world, they reject the fruits of Tibetan civilization in favor of the newest technology and the most spectacular entertainments. Like other peoples thrust into modernity, they are choosing the values of samsara, unable to recognize the negative consequences of this choice. The traditional teachings would help them see that when they act in this way, they are like someone attempting to satisfy his thirst by drinking saltwater. But the foundation that would enable them to take these teachings to heart has been undermined. Today even knowledge of the classical language in which Buddhist texts are preserved is beginning to wane, for the Tibetan taught in schools is so filled with new terms coined to adapt to present trends that the words of the Dharma—and the meanings they once transmitted—will soon be forgotten.

Unlike the external difficulties against which the Tibetan refugee community had to struggle in the early days, these changes have accumulated gradually, and almost invisibly. Yet in the end they may undermine much of the good work that Tibetans in exile have been able to accomplish, precisely because they subtly drain away the vitality of the tradition in ways few people would even notice. One possible sign of this danger is a growing sense of fragmentation within the exile community. In the early days, the Tibetans who had escaped the takeover of their homeland felt united by the common tragedy that had befallen them, and all worked together for the sake of the whole. Little by little, however, this sense of cooperation began to give way. First the divisions among the schools began to assert themselves, then divisions based on geographic regions in Tibet. Today there is even fragmentation on the basis of specific personalities.

On the other hand, there are some grounds for optimism. The plight of the Tibetan community has become increasingly well-known in the world at large. This global visibility may help Tibetans in exile maintain a sense of their own shared identity and aims. Tibetans are also well aware that many individuals from the most highly developed countries are drawn to Tibetan Buddhism. It is possible that this interest will encourage Tibetans to seek out the value in their own tradition.

Finally, since winning the Nobel Peace Prize more than a decade ago, His Holiness The Dalai Lama has become a symbol of peace around the globe, and his message of loving compassion has found a welcome reception everywhere. Through his influence, the Tibetans are regarded as a people of peace and goodwill. This regard places expectations upon us that may inspire our actions. We can only hope that in the years to come the unparalleled success of His Holiness in representing the Tibetan people in the forum of world opinion will translate into the restoration of Tibetan rights and the Tibetan homeland, the goals for which all Tibetan people so deeply yearn.

Beyond the Borders of Tibet

Whatever its effects on the Tibetan people, the Tibetan diaspora has had a positive impact on Buddhism in other parts of Asia and also in the West. In the Himalayan lands of Ladakh, Lahul, Spiti, Sikkim, Bhutan, and Nepal, places where a

Tibetan form of Buddhism was already being practiced, the dispersion of Tibetan teachers has reinforced and strengthened the local traditions.
Tibetan lamas who established new Dharma centers
in exile have been able to share their knowledge
with students from these lands. The community of
lamas has also been able to reach out to similar
communities in other cultures that follow the
Tibetan traditions. At the annual Monlam Chenmo
in Bodh Gayā, for example, lamas and laypeople
from many countries where the Nyingma teachings
have taken hold are able to gather each year, renewing their faith and finding inspiration to develop the
Dharma more strongly in their own lands.

On a global scale, the consequences of the
Tibetan diaspora have been more dramatic. Quite
unexpectedly, the tragic destruction wrought in
Tibet has meant that the blessings of the Dharma as
it was practiced in Tibet have spread around the
globe. The teachers who fled Tibet in the 1950s and
1960s soon came in contact with individuals interested in the Dharma as it had been practiced in
Tibet. The resulting dynamic has now led to the
founding of Dharma centers in all parts of the world,
together with programs for translating Dharma-
related works into scores of different languages.

In Europe, Russia, and the Americas, in
Australia and New Zealand, Taiwan, Malaysia, and
Singapore, Buddhism is known and admired, and
the Mahāyāna has found a receptive audience. In

all these lands new to Tibetan Buddhist teachings, stupas have been built, Buddhist texts have become available for study, and retreat centers and institutions for intensive study and practice have opened their doors. The teachings of Padmasambhava, which seem so timely in this troubled age, have generated particular interest.

The numerous teachers from Tibet (and from other Buddhist lands) who today travel widely in Asia and the West, the small number who have actually taken up residence in new lands, the thousands of Buddhist texts that have been published in Western languages: All these are like ripples in a pond, slowly spreading outward. Individuals all over the world have realized that Buddhism has teachings that can benefit everyone, and that the Dharma addresses issues that have universal application.

Of course, many people who visit Dharma centers do so initially out of curiosity, hoping to learn techniques for easing tension or finding some resolution to their problems. Yet even if their interest is not based on much knowledge, even if they only practice a short time, the influence on their lives can be lasting and the benefit great. It is not just that there are more Buddhists in the West now, or that Buddhism is more visible or more fashionable. Rather, this interest can now develop from a basic understanding that Buddhism is a serious tradition of knowledge and practice. Westerners are beginning to see that Buddhism offers a fresh approach to inquiry and a wide range of methods and perspectives for individual growth, for answering questions about the meaning of life, and for gaining greater peace of mind. There is a genuine appreciation for the Dharma, even among those who have only limited contact with authentic Buddhist teachers, and this appreciation can lead to a more mature and beneficial understanding.

The freedom of religion practiced in America and elsewhere has supported these changes, for each person is free to question old approaches and beliefs—a stark contrast to the authoritarianism under which the people of Tibet presently live. The non-dogmatic approach of Buddhism itself fits in well with this free world.

As newly formed Dharma centers have widened their circles of students, there has been a positive effect on society at large. On the social level, there seems to be more compassion for the suffering of others. On the intellectual level, scientists, educators, philosophers, and psychologists, aware that the Buddhist tradition has much to offer even in the most complex fields of knowledge, seem more open to new ideas and interdisciplinary approaches. On the personal level, individuals increasingly recognize the importance of such practices as mindfulness, meditation, compassion, and loving kindness. The Buddha's Four Noble Truths are being recast in ways that allow people from many walks of life to look at their circumstances with greater honesty and clarity. Finally, there are religious leaders in almost every tradition who freely acknowledge that the centuries-old traditions of inquiry, accumulated wisdom, and disciplined moral conduct transmitted in Buddhist lands may be able to infuse their own teachings with new vitality.

But if the Dharma is to take root in the West, it seems essential that the traditions engage their Western students on a level that enables their disciples to manifest the full blessings of the teachings. While the number of practitioners is increasing, the Dharma is still very new in the West. Great gaps in view and ways of understanding between traditional teachers and their students remain, and the very warmth of their interactions may foster assumptions that mask the extent of these gaps. In this situation, the question remains: Can the traditions communicate fully the special qualities of the Dharma and the depth of its meaning? Or might students be satisfied with the outer forms of the Dharma, and fail to connect with the teachings in a way that gives these forms meaning and purpose?

Communicating the Blessings: The Central Role of Tradition

The Buddhist approach to the fundamental issues that have always engaged humanity differs in key respects from Western ways of thinking. Unlike Western philosophy, the Dharma emphasizes non-conceptual forms of knowledge. Unlike Western religions, it accepts neither a creator God nor an unchanging, eternal soul, and holds that we are all directly responsible for developing our highest potential as human beings.

Unlike Western psychology, the Dharma does not accept the ordinary workings of mind—even in their most refined state—as the final word on human capacities. And unlike science, the Dharma rejects the sharp separation of the mental and physical realms. It tells us on the one hand that the principles of causality extend far beyond what science now acknowledges, and it maintains on the other hand that the laws of cause and effect, or karma, are valid only as long as one adheres to a specific view of self and world and dismisses the possibility of knowledge based on a different understanding. These distinctions are fundamental for individuals who wish to clarify in their own mind the unique attributes of Buddhism. Then they can with confidence explain to others the teachings that make Buddhism a worthwhile field of study for the West.

Preparing for Transmission

The Buddha taught that samsara—the way we ordinarily live—follows the laws of cause and effect, and that until we understand those laws, we have no possibility for making a radical break with the patterns of suffering we have constructed. Buddhism teaches that those patterns can be identified and understood, and that such knowledge makes it possible to diagnose the root cause of our suffering and apply the antidote, just as a doctor would apply the proper medicine to cure a disease.

From a Buddhist perspective, the key to bringing about real and lasting change in our lives is to investigate the universal patterns that shape our experience, the workings of the mind, and the conditions of our lives. First comes the realization that samsara is characterized by suffering and frustration, and that the laws governing its operation are pitiless in undermining our deepest aspirations and longings. Next we learn to recognize how samsara is created and sustained by the actions of body and mind and the relationship we establish between the self and its world. We see that we have programmed ourselves to repeat the same cycles of suffering over and over, and we learn that while it is easy to get caught in samsara, it is almost impossible to escape. Gradually we discover that the teachings on pratītya-samutpāda (interdependent origination), offer the knowledge we need to devise a better program for ourselves, one that will enable us to escape the traps that samsara sets. Armed with this knowledge, we can reverse these destructive conditions and attain the goal of enlightenment.

The Buddha first presented the teachings that can free us from samsara after attaining enlightenment under the Bodhi Tree at Bodh Gayā. In the Deer Park at Sārnāth, he taught the fundamental insights that have guided Buddhists everywhere for twenty-five centuries. Later he presented the depth of his realization in the profound teachings of the Prajñāpāramitā, the foundation for the Mahāyāna tradition. These works, many of which are still available, offer a precise road map that shows, step by step, how to travel the path to liberation and enlightenment. The śāstras (commentary tradition) of India, developed and refined over the course of a thousand years, added to this treasury of knowledge, as great masters explained how to apply the teachings and helped clarify their meaning for others.

Having the teachings of the Dharma available gives human beings a precious opportunity, one we cannot afford to lose. At present, we may not be ready to take full advantage of this opportunity, for the words that could accurately bring the Dharma into Western languages do not yet seem to be available. However, this is beginning to change. In the near future, as the realization of new Dharma students matures, they may well develop ways to present the Buddhist path in forms appropriate to the modern world. The more fully students investigate the teachings, explore their meaning, and follow the path they lay out, the more readily the conditions for this transmission can be set in place for the benefit of all.

Relying on the Tradition

Individuals drawn to serious study and practice of the Dharma today have tremendous resources available to them. Buddhist centers have been founded all over the world, and thousands of books on Buddhism have been published. Scores of teachers travel widely, offering instruction and blessings. Thirty years ago the basic vocabulary and concepts of the Dharma were quite foreign to the West, but today terms such as karma, Dharma, mantra, mandala, nirvana, and samsara are quite familiar, at least in certain circles. Dharma ways of thinking are beginning to have an impact as well, so that the vision of the Buddha can be communicated with greater accuracy. Those who come in contact with the teachings can see more readily and with less chance of distortion how the practice of Buddhism might reshape and improve their own lives.

However, this greater accessibility also carries with it a considerable risk. Someone may study and practice up to a point, but may assume prematurely that he or she has sufficient understanding to reinterpret traditional teachings. Since interpretations based on less than complete understanding tend to accord with one's culturally conditioned views and personal ways of thinking, the real meaning of the Dharma can easily be lost, buried in a heap of explanations and reformulations that 'fit' better with the views of the audience. This risk is particularly pronounced for those who have a personal or professional stake in presenting the Dharma; for instance, for someone who likes the idea of becoming 'the teacher', 'the master,' or 'the professor.'

The Dharma certainly does not belong to any one group of people or country, and anyone is free to study and practice it. But in countries where Buddhism is still very new, it seems ill-advised for students to imagine that their own understanding or interpretation of the teachings has the same validity as interpretations accepted by Dharma practitioners down through the centuries.

Perhaps the traditional interpretations are not to everyone's liking, but that does not mean they should be rejected. Students who try to turn the Dharma into what they think it ought to be are likely to do harm: to themselves, to the tradition, and to those who stand to benefit if the inner meaning of the teachings can successfully be preserved and transmitted. If Buddhism is reinterpreted before practitioners are able to prove the value of traditional approaches in their own experience, the result may be to promote ignorance over knowledge.

Modern ways of thinking often assume that the past has little to offer the present and view the newest ideas as the best ideas. Dharma students who adopt this perspective are likely to imagine that many traditional teachings were meant for another time and place and are no longer relevant. They may maintain, for example, that certain aspects of the teachings are unnecessarily complex, culture-bound, or unduly scholastic.

Applied to the Dharma, this way of thinking soon leads to confusion and distortion. Even individuals convinced of the great value of the Dharma may unwittingly twist it to advance their own ideas, confirm their own values, or serve their own purposes. Many who are most eager to borrow techniques or ideas from Buddhism are unwilling to engage the tradition on its own terms. How sad if such attitudes were to lead to discarding or radically altering the map of spiritual realization that the scriptures lay out in such beautiful detail!

When Dharma students seek to make use of the teachings rather than follow them with respect, they unwittingly undermine the power of the teachings. Once this has happened, those who come to the Dharma for guidance may go away disappointed or disillusioned, losing a wonderful opportunity to transform their lives.

For someone caught up in the rational mindset that Westerners generally depend on, it may seem a relatively simple manner to decide which teachings have value and which can be rejected. But these distinctions are actually a product of a particular and limited approach to knowledge. Like other people throughout history, Westerners tend to reject knowledge that they do not understand. Even individuals who recognize the limited value of scientific methods in many domains are still guided at a subtle level by the criteria for truth that science has set in place. Instead of being rational in the sense of 'wise, reasonable, sensible, and sound', they cling to notions of rationality that may not apply to the spiritual path. Relying on familiar patterns of knowing, they choose a course that can more easily obscure new knowledge rather than bring it to light.

Given these tendencies, so subtle and difficult to detect, it is best to be cautious before revising or rejecting the traditional teachings. Words and meanings can always be twisted, but karma cannot. If the result of acting on our own beliefs is that we discard the very teachings that could have taken us beyond ourselves and our limitations, we will have chosen a foolish course indeed.

If Westerners truly wish to shape their own trustworthy form of Buddhism, let them resolve to devote extensive effort to study and practice of the tradition. Let them learn through their own experience and reflection the inner meaning of the teachings, the significance of the language found in the texts, and the power of the symbols and rituals. Until this happens, it seems better to keep the tradition as it has been handed down essentially intact.

The Place of Initiations and Rituals

Many individuals drawn to Tibetan Buddhism seem to be especially interested in rituals and initiations, which they associate with the esoteric aspect of the teachings. Having read or heard a little about Tantra, they arrive at Tibetan centers or attend teachings for the express purpose of receiving empowerment and initiation from lamas whom they otherwise know little about. Observing this, my students and friends have often asked me why I do not offer initiations. Sometimes the question is put differently: Do I believe that participating in rituals on this basis has value for new Dharma students?

In Tibet, the circumstances under which initiations could be given were clear. Apart from simple ceremonies performed as a blessing or for longevity, each initiation required several specific forms of preparation or commitment on the part of the person wishing to receive it. First, in all four schools of Tibetan Buddhism, initiations that involved the four abhiṣekas (consecrations) were open only to applicants who had completed well-defined preliminary practices. In the Nyingma school, these preliminary practices would have included completion

of the 'bum-lnga, the five 'hundred thousand' practices that begin with a hundred thousand prostra-
tions. Second, before receiving empowerment, the
initiate would have to agree to do the practices associated with the initiation every day for the rest of his
or her life. This requirement invoked the power of
the initiation as an aid in the growth of śamathā
(calm) and vipaśyana (clear insight). In particular,
the core practices of mantra and visualization were
considered the gateway to higher samādhis that
could accelerate progress on the path toward realization. Finally, the initiate took certain vows specific
to the Mantrayāna.

The fourteen fundamental vows of the Mantrayāna invoke the power of kāya, vācā, and citta, the
body, speech, and mind of the Enlightened Ones.
They were considered far more binding than the
vows a a monk would take on receiving ordination.
Since breaking these vows or discontinuing the
practices might cause harm to the initiate and also
to the teacher, it was vital that the initiate have a
clear understanding of what was involved and a
firm resolve to honor the commitments. Otherwise,
the power of the initiation would be lost and there
could be very negative consequences.

In the modern world, such traditional safeguards
are not well understood, and the enthusiasm of students new to the Dharma can blind them to their
importance. Confident of their own good intentions,
they may not take seriously the warnings in the

texts that breaking even a single vow or commitment has severe repercussions. Not deeply familiar with the changeability of the mind, they may take on commitments that they later find themselves unwilling or unable to keep. Perhaps the worst case is when students—and I have known some myself—participate in an initiation without understanding its nature and purpose, and are told afterwards that they have now taken on serious commitments that they break at their own peril.

The importance of the restrictions and requirements that accompany ritual practice in Tibetan Buddhism cannot readily be explained on the rational level. Insight depends on direct realization, which cannot be quickly conveyed or bestowed by someone else. That is one reason for the requirement that a person seeking initiation must first complete the preliminary practices. This preparation helps instill respect for the significance of initiation, which passes on teachings central to the lineage of awakening. Although Westerners sometimes seem to believe that their situation is exceptional, and that this implies that traditional ways of following the Dharma do not apply to them, the formal safeguards have a purpose. Both students and teachers should consider this purpose very carefully before deciding to set these safeguards aside.

For a Dharma student who receives initiations after careful preparation and then practices with the guidance of a qualified teacher, the inner meaning of the teachings gradually reveals itself. Keeping the commitments supports this process of deepening insight, protecting practitioners so that they do not fall back into the grip of karma and the kleśas. When students lack a thorough preparation, they do not have this kind of protection.

Traditionally, initiation ceremonies were occasions for the transfer of specific powers, similar to the ancient ceremonies of coronation through which a prince would ascend to the rule of the kingdom. The transfer is also a transformation, and the world that the initiate enters by means of the initiation is truly a different place, governed by different rules and even a different logic. If this transforming power is diluted, so that the initiation becomes a change of condition in name only, who will even realize what has been lost?

The modern outlook on life encourages innovation and experimentation, and this seems to work well in many areas. Initiations, however, operate on a symbolic level that connects the initiate with the enlightened lineage. Since a symbolic action, once taken, cannot be undone, experimentation does not support the logic that gives coherence and meaning to symbolic actions. People who are reluctant to progress toward commitment may imagine that they are practicing the Dharma, but is this really so?

In reflecting on these matters, it is clear that the teacher bears the primary responsibility, for the student cannot be expected to understand what is at stake. If the teacher does not fully prepare the student, explaining the background of the initiation, the nature of the commitments being made, and the importance of honoring those commitments, the student cannot be expected to think seriously about whether this is an appropriate step. Yet the texts state clearly that once a student has taken on the vows and commitments that an initiation imposes, there is no easy way to 'give them back'.

Some say there are good reasons for changing the traditional approach and relaxing the traditional safeguards. In the present kaliyuga, the dark era when all that has value is in decline, it may not be realistic to expect the formal requirements of an initiation to be upheld. The practice lineages themselves are in jeopardy, perhaps even on the verge of disappearing entirely, and Mantrayāna practices are being widely introduced in foreign lands. Some say that, given these special circumstances, it may be appropriate to treat an initiation as though it were a simple blessing rather than an abhiṣeka.

Yet I am not so certain. Before accepting these arguments, it would seem important to make a thorough search of the texts—and there are thousands of them—that discuss initiation, to see whether there is any authority for relaxing the time-honored protections in special circumstances. Such authoritative support would help relieve concerns that these changes may accelerate decline of the Dharma rather than foster its transmission.

There is a Tibetan story about a 'lama' who gave a wealthy patron very rare and advanced teachings. When his benefactor expressed his deep thanks, made offerings, and praised his teacher, the 'lama' replied, "You, too are worthy of praise as a great patron of the Dharma. That is why I have given you these teachings, even though I myself have not kept their lineage and do not understand their meaning." I am concerned that similar situations may be occurring as the Mantrayāna enters new lands.

If a teacher does intend to give an initiation as simply a ceremonial blessing, students should be made aware of this, for otherwise they may have unrealistic expectations that can lead to disappointment. They should also be instructed that they have a part to play in activating the teachings, lest they blame the lineage or the Dharma when difficulties arise in their practice or results do not manifest.

For the student who has developed sincere and stable faith in the Dharma, a firm connection to the lineage, and strong compassion toward others— the student who is without doubt—initiations may be deeply inspiring and form the foundation for a path of practice that can mature for a long time to come. If a student also has the continuing support of a qualified teacher who is willing to review the student's practice and attainment, there are sure to be real benefits. If these elements are lacking, however, this way of approaching the path may not be appropriate.

There are many important Buddhist teachings that do not depend on initiations or esoteric teachings that can be taught to anone with complete confidence. Taking refuge in Buddha, Dharma, and Sangha, learning meditation, chanting mantra, completing the preliminary practices, and cultivating the four thoughts that orient the mind to liberation are all ways to stabilize and calm the mind that provide access to the Dharma and can revolutionize ordinary consciousness. Anyone may also find the Bodhicaryāvatāra, Kun-bzang Bla-ma'i Zhal-lung, and Path of Heroes, as well as other śāstras and teachings on Abhidharma deeply illuminating.

For students who strongly wish for traditional initiations, there are many prayers and meditations for which the hearing lineage is available, as well as one or two basic practices such as Guru Yoga. These prayers and meditative exercises, as well as practices that focus on the Buddha, on Guru Rinpoche, on Avalokiteśvara, or on Mañjuśrī are wholly appropriate and effective for developing insight, wisdom, and compassion. In this sense, Buddhism truly offers something for everyone.

Those of us familiar with the tradition have a special obligation to clarify the power and value of these fundamental practices and doctrines that are available to benefit all beings. If we can do this, perhaps the fascination with ritual and initiations evident in some circles today will gradually resolve into a more balanced perspective.

Placing Ritual in Perspective

In traditional Buddhist practice, devotional practice, faith, and moving liturgy all go hand in hand with careful analytic inquiry and penetrating insight. Ritual is not conducted for its own sake or because of the power it may be thought to confer; instead, it is integrated with meditative practice and rigorous intellectual study to make a unified whole.

In countries without a real Dharma tradition, this same encompassing framework is missing. I have seen individuals sincere in their attraction to the Dharma who are convinced that what matters in the conduct of ritual is the sensations that performing the ritual may evoke. But the sense of heightened awareness—the 'good vibes' that ritual may bring—are not the essential element of such practice at all. The Buddha himself warned against relying on ritual as a substitute for realization, and that warning seems to me to apply very directly in our present times.

Appreciation for elevated feelings can be very positive. But when individuals depend on the 'spiritual entertainment value' of their practice to keep themselves motivated, they are selling the Dharma short. When their positive feelings fade, as will happen, their grounding in the teachings is not likely to be strong enough to sustain them. Where a whole community emphasizes this kind of motivation, serious, well-intentioned individuals who come to the teachings in search of clarity and insight will feel out of place. Most likely they will turn away, dissatisfied and even disillusioned.

As Dharma students learn to appreciate the philosophical and psychological insights that give ritual its inner meaning, practices such as pūjā (ritual ceremonies) and initiations will be seen for what they are: invitations to enter the mandala of realization through actions that integrate the wisdom of body, speech, and mind. At that point, ritual adds another dimension to the reality of enlightened realization, offering a powerful method for transcending the limits of the ordinary mind. But at present, the background that would allow for understanding the true meaning of ritual has yet to be established in the West. The vocabulary is not available, the symbols that ritual evokes are little understood, and the attitudes that would reveal the deeper significance of ritual conduct are not fully formed.

In contemporary culture, intellectual insight was long ago divorced from religious devotion. Today most people find it natural to separate the two. Serious Dharma students who feel a heart connection to the teachings have absorbed this way of thinking, but that does not make it right. The task that we should set ourselves is to rediscover how to integrate ritual with meditative clarity and analytic inquiry. Until this happens, it may be better not to place too great an emphasis on such rituals as initiation, even when they seem to forge a link to the tradition. Ritual alone, without analysis and medi-

tative inquiry, is like poetry translated from a foreign language: Its rich dimensions of meaning and
significance can only be approximated, and misin-
terpretation or undervaluation is likely.

This is not to say that one way is definitely better
than another. With Buddhism entering new cultures that are not fully prepared to receive it, there
is a need to respond to the circumstances that present themselves and adapt the teachings and methods accordingly. As new seeds are planted in the soil
of a new culture, a few healthy shoots may sprout;
properly cared for, they may eventually bear rich
fruit. Yet my own sense is that we must move cau-
tiously, and that is the course that we have followed
in our own community. If we are too free in experi-
menting, the integrity and power of the Dharma may
be compromised, and that would be too great a
price to pay. I hope that the advanced masters active
today will continue to reflect deeply on this issue
before determining how to proceed, weighing the
karmic consequences of each course of action.

There is another reason to act with special care
with regard to ritual. The good will with which
Buddhism has generally been received by modern
societies conceals a certain lack of comprehension.
In today's world, the power of karma and kleśa is
not even questioned or challenged, so how can one
expect real appreciation for the teachings that serve
as their antidote? When questions relating to the
purpose of human existence are generally dismissed

as topics for the idle and the chronically discontented, how can there be respect for a tradition that takes such issues as central?

Given the lack of comprehension that still characterizes Western attitudes toward Buddhism, it would be wrong to read too much into the friendly attitudes that many people express toward Dharma. My own sense is that scientists, Western religious leaders, and thoughtful individuals from all walks of life welcome Buddhism only up to a certain point, as a sane, peaceful, tolerant, and ethically honorable tradition. Beyond that point, they tend to dismiss its ultimate significance, and their skeptical outlook even inclines them to be hostile.

If such persons understand ritual as akin to idol worship or dismiss it as superstition, the cause of the Dharma will be damaged. If they interpret it as a more exotic version of the same dogmatic beliefs that many Westerners have rejected in their own religious traditions, the door to appreciating the special qualities of the Buddha's teachings will slam shut. And if people who claim to have received initiation into the highest teachings do not display the qualities that come with greater realization, their actions will only play into the hands of those who stand ready to discount the significance and value of the enlightened lineage.

Among those drawn to the Dharma, too strong a focus on initiation and other rituals raises a different set of concerns. Anyone who has the impression that attending certain kinds of initiations or 'obtaining' specific teachings will guarantee quick spiritual progress is almost certain to be disappointed. If such individuals take on commitments lightly and give them up without considering the consequences, they may damage their connection to the Dharma and contribute, however unintentionally, to weakening the tradition.

With these concerns in mind, I hope that at least students are clearly informed about their own responsibilities whenever they attend initiations or receive other traditional teachings. If possible, I hope that their training begins with a comprehensive and coherent introduction to the Dharma. Once they appreciate ritual as a means of expressing and supporting other aspects of the teachings, and understand more clearly all that is involved in activating the dynamic of the Buddhist path, they can choose for themselves how to shape their practice. That, at least, is the course that I have tried to set for the members of our community.

Reflections on Rebirth

Viewed as a form of dogma, Buddhist teachings on rebirth can be a stumbling block for Westerners interested in the Dharma. Historically, Plato and other Western thinkers accepted the reality of rebirth, and even in Christianity many of the early Church Fathers believed that an individual could be born more than once. Although today rebirth is regarded as somewhat of a fringe idea and is generally dismissed by mainstream thinkers, there is no obvious reason why this should be so. If human beings have the power to go to heaven after death, as Western religions generally teach, why should they not have the power to take new birth?

Rebirth is a teaching integral to Buddhism; accepting this teaching and contemplating its significance lays the foundation for compassion to arise and manifest in enlightened action. Even to people who do not yet comprehend its importance to their spiritual growth, this teaching makes good sense when they begin to understand the power of mind. For instance, most people can recall times when a strong experience during the day shaped the content of the dreams they had that night, or even for months afterward. In the same way, it seems that experiences in one life could shape the consciousness that takes form in the next life. It also seems possible that patterns established by the mind could transmit themselves forward even when the physical continuity that characterizes a single life ceases to operate. Like perennials in a garden that die away and then grow back, different forms of life may arise and succeed one another without depending on the same physical form.

The ability of the mind to sustain both waking reality and the very different reality of dreams only hints at its remarkable power. From a Buddhist perspective, mind is the foundation for both samsara and nirvana, the soil in which karma and the positive qualities of the human spirit can take root. Mind as it operates in samsara has one quality, but mind as it develops on the path is very different in its nature, and the mind of enlightenment is wholly different again.

Ordinarily we limit our understanding of the mind to the way it functions in receiving and processing thoughts and images and initiating actions. But there are deeper, more mysterious levels of mind that we can learn to access through meditation. Here we can chart a definite sequence. As the meditating mind lets go of its ordinary patterns, it actually becomes meditation. After that, it becomes prajñā, or transcendent wisdom; eventually it becomes all-knowing—the enlightened state.

This broader perspective on the potentialities of mind helps explain why most of us do not remember our past lives. In the bardo, the state between one life and the next, consciousness is completely different from what we know at present. During the nine months we spend in the womb, it is different again. As we move through these other realities, the rhythms of time itself are transformed. Whatever has come before recedes into obscurity, much as a person who is dreaming usually does not remember his or her life while awake.

Mind and Objective Reality

The chief argument against rebirth is that mind depends on the brain and the physical body, so that it could not continue to function once the body dies. But this view is based on certain assumptions about the relationship of mind to reality that may be accurate only from a limited perspective.

We are used to thinking of the mind as the subjective knower of an independent, objective world that we experience through the senses. It is this subjective mind that seems bound to the body. But if we gain knowledge of the objective world only through mental operations, how can we say that objective 'reality' is prior to or independent of the mind? If we let go of this presupposition and look at what we actually experience, we realize that the distinction between subjective mind and objective reality is itself a mental construct. Contrary to our usual understanding that raw sensory data precedes mental operations, mind makes its interpretations at the very outset. Only as these interpretations are fed into the process of perception does the objective, apparent world become available for the subjective knower to know as such.

Before the structures of subject and object take hold, there is simply mind reading mind, in an endless circle. The resulting readouts are the perceived world, along with the one who perceives it. Within this reflexive system, 'objective reality' presents itself, but this reality belongs to the physical realm where the body, but not the mind, appears. Thus a particular version of what counts as true or real can never establish itself independently of the mind that identifies it. The whole display that is our 'objective reality' is a magical exhibition of mind, a kind of infinite interplay that is self-manifesting and self-perpetuating. Since this is so, to say that the mind depends on the body is a vast oversimplification.

Ordinary consciousness will continue to see mind as linked to the body, because for that consciousness, the polarity of self and world is a given. From the very beginning we have acted and interpreted in this way, and by now we are conditioned by past interpretations and reactions to continue to produce the same polarized understanding. If we take the traditional image of the Wheel of Life as a model for this conditioned operation, the patterns through which mind projects a subjective knower and a known world could be considered spokes of the wheel, whirled into existence by 'previous' projections. Turning repeatedly without interruption, the momentum of their creation contributes the transitions that perpetuate the whole.

At this level, belief in rebirth depends on seeing that the laws of karma—rigid, inescapable, infinitely powerful—do not depend on a physical matrix to operate. The analysis we have been making here supports this insight, for it suggests that mind, not 'objective reality', is primary. Traditionally, this primacy of mind is described in terms of the interaction of karma with the kleśas, the emotional obscurations that rule the operation of mind. The kleśa-ridden mind generates actions and ways of perceiving that shape and determine the world into which such actions manifest.

Karma is at once the depositing of the consequences of past action and the generating of new actions that will be deposited in turn. Its operation marks the transition or transformation of mental patternings into consequences that are both mental and physical (as conventional mind understands these categories). And there is no reason at all that these transformations must be circumscribed by a specific set of physical constraints: 'this body', 'this life', 'my present existence'.

Yet this level of insight leaves us at the mercy of karmic patterns, including the karma that governs rebirth. Though it breaks through a certain limiting interpretation of subject/object interactions, it continues to accept that for the cause and effect structures of karma to operate, something of substance must be produced and passed on.

The Buddhist teaching of śūnyatā, often (but misleadingly) translated as emptiness, suggests that this cannot be the whole picture. If we reflect on the dynamic of self-projection that shapes our experience, we can see what is missing. If karma and its consequences result entirely from the operation of mind, then karma—even though it appears as infinitely powerful in its workings—is utterly open. The teaching of pratītyasamutpāda, which lays out the dynamic through which thoughts and appearances arise, clarifies the interplay of our ordinary perspective and śūnyatā, revealing that śūnyatā and the workings of karma are two ways of pointing at the same operation of mind.

Ordinary mind, operating with its categories of 'is/is not' and 'have/have not' will insist on the rigid, dualistic structures that make karma inescapable. But it is possible to penetrate these structures by cultivating the conceptual realization that beyond them lies a unity that is all-embracing. Once formed, this concept can become the gateway to a meditative exploration of mind. When we learn how to activate it, meditation operates mind differently. Meditation has the power to channel insight toward a deep creativity, not bound either by dualistic structures that accept the objectively real as an inalterable given, or by the onrushing momentum of karma. Liberated from the restraints of dualistic structures, the power of insight has unimaginable beauty, for it illuminates a knowledge that is close to enlightenment itself, and it leads to action drawn unfailingly toward the welfare of all beings.

By refining the power of mind that meditation reveals and activates, we can learn for ourselves how to transform the operation of mind. We can build bridges from one way of being to another, very different way. When we can see directly how consciousness, perception, thoughts, and cognition cooperate to activate the impulses that manifest as karma and kleśa, we can control these patternings.

Initially, this understanding might manifest in a greater ability to control the way that the mind generates thoughts or gets caught in habitual patterns, or in learning how to take a more active role in the reality of dreams. Gradually, we learn to shape the way that experience arises for us from moment to moment and day to day. Eventually, we gain insight into how the same patterns play themselves out across many lifetimes. As meditative awareness stabilizes, we can develop the ability to maintain such awareness even in the face of highly disruptive events—including death, which might be considered the most disruptive event of all. At that point it becomes possible to control the process of rebirth.

As an analogy for how this could be, consider the place you are presently located. Right now it is solid land, but at some point in the past it may have been ocean. In order for this transition to take place, space had to accommodate both alternatives: land and ocean.

In the same way, mind can accommodate different alternatives—different lifetimes. And it can accommodate them without being something substantial in itself. In Buddhist teachings, there is no need to tie the ability to direct the process to a 'someone' who is reborn, to a 'soul', an 'atman', or a 'self'. What is required is determination and resolve, coupled with the kind of meditative realization that gives control over the powers of the mind.

The knowledge of how to control the mind to shape the process of rebirth has been passed on by the great lineage holders of the past. There are works that describe in detail practices for taking rebirth knowingly and how to perfect and refine this capacity of mind through meditation much as a chemist might use chemical reactions possible only under rarified conditions to create a new molecule. As the Bar-do Thos-grol (best known in the West as *The Book of the Dead*) demonstrates, the Nyingma school places special emphasis on such teachings. But this power is by no means an end in itself. What ultimately matters is cultivating the more fundamental power of mind to shape experience as either samsara or nirvana. At that point, we can create a living paradise, free ourselves completely from the laws of karma, and reveal mind itself as śūnyatā.

The Phenomenon of Tulkus

Throughout history Buddhist masters have used the power over rebirth that realization brings to manifest in ways that benefit other beings. One of these skillful means is the continuation of tulku (sprul-sku) lineages, through which a great master deliberately chooses to take rebirth from one life to the next. It is an aspect of the tradition that seems to fascinate Westerners, and I am often asked about it.

The 'modern' tulku tradition in Tibet traces back to Guru Padmasambhava and his twenty-five principal disciples and continues to the present day. Rong-zom Mahāpandita, who lived in the eleventh century, is a famous example of this tradition. As a child, this great master demonstrated a knowledge so vast and profound that he was taken to meet the renowned Indian pandita Atīśa, who at that time had just arrived in Tibet. When it was proposed that the child engage Atīśa in debate, Atīśa refused, saying that Rong-zom was the incarnation of his own teacher, the Mahāsiddha Krsna-pa, and it would not be respectful for Atīśa to debate with him.

In the thirteenth century, the great Kagyu master Karma Paksi gave his disciple O-rgyan-pa some precious belongings and told him to care for them until his return in the next life, after which he passed away. His reincarnation was Rang-'byung rDo-rje. Sometimes it is said that this transmission marked the establishment of the first formal incarnation lineage. Since then there have been many recognized incarnation lineages in all schools of Tibetan Buddhism, including the lineage of Dalai Lamas, first acknowledged in the sixteenth century. Many tulkus born into these lineages have made profound and remarkable contributions to the Dharma and have benefited countless beings. Events in the lives of these outstanding tulkus, including the circumstances of their rediscovery, are famous throughout the Tibetan tradition.

Tibet's system of tulkus, which is unique among Buddhist lands, has played a very important role in the transmission of the teachings from generation to generation. Tulkus have often been highly gifted individuals with remarkable knowledge, qualities, and willingness to serve the Dharma from an early age. From childhood on they are given intensive training that refines qualities of compassion and wisdom and instills deep respect for the Buddha, Dharma, and Sangha. Sometimes they seem to have a kind of knowledge that surpasses ordinary human capacities, as if it belonged to the lineage itself.

Still, many find it difficult to take seriously the claim that one individual can actually be reborn over and over. Even if they do accept this notion in principle, they still wonder whether everyone who is identified as a tulku should be accepted as such, especially when some tulkus appear to act in ways that go counter to the Dharma.

Most Westerners, and even some Tibetans, may not understand the full implications of the term 'tulku'. Literally, 'tulku' means 'manifesting body'; applied to a person, it identifies that individual as having the ability to control the place and circumstances of rebirth. According to traditional Mahāyāna texts, this ability emerges over the course of the first eight stages of the Bodhisattva path.

To place this in context, consider that even on the first stage, a Bodhisattva is said to have 1,200 incredible qualities of noble-mindedness, skill, and power to manifest as necessary to aid beings. By the eighth stage, known as The Immovable, the Bodhisattva has gained innumerable spiritual qualities and capacities. These include the ten powers, among which are the power to completely control mind and karma, and thus rebirth. At this point the Bodhisattva is capable of emanating as many forms as needed to liberate others. The Daśabhūmika Sūtra and the Madhyamakāvatāra of the great philosopher Candrakīrti are among the numerous texts that discuss these teachings in detail.

Relying on these descriptions might seem to give us a basis for attempting to observe and evaluate lamas who bear the title of tulku, to determine whether they can be considered authentic holders of their incarnation lineage. If we were to follow that course, few individuals could claim the title. However, we must be cautious not to judge too quickly. As the Buddha himself warned, until we have obtained the omniscience of the enlightened ones, we cannot rely completely on our perceptions and judgments concerning others.

It may also help to bear in mind that tulkus can appear in various ways. While some tulkus choose the circumstances of their rebirth, others are compelled to take a particular rebirth by the complexities of karma (for instance, as evoked through the power of their prayers in past lives). Others take rebirth to fulfill certain duties or serve the purposes of others. Thus, a wide range of individuals of varying capacities may hold the title of tulku.

The incredibly rigorous path of the Bodhisattva is not the only way to gain control over karma. Consciousness that is highly trained in the methods of the Mantrayāna may pass quickly through stages of the Bodhisattva path that might otherwise take many aeons to accomplish. The Bar-do Thos-grol, for instance, tells us that certain kinds of meditation practice bestow the knowledge and power needed to control experience. More fundamental still, Dharma practices that purify karma and the kleśas affect the whole being, and when perfected they become a source of power or merit that can guide rebirth. Beyond the power of prayers and positive karma, there is also the power of skillful means, based on meditation and visualization, and tulkus who manifest on this basis are also known in the tradition.

While the question of whether someone is truly a tulku can be difficult to answer with the ordinary mind, sometimes an individual's exceptional action is its own authentication. As the Buddha said in the Sūtras, whether one's heart belongs to the family of Bodhisattvas will become clear through the way one manifests in word and deed. In the case of tulkus, serving the Dharma and aiding sentient beings is part of a tulku's purpose for being born. When an individual takes up this responsibility and fulfills this purpose, this kind of selfless and purposeful action provides evidence that on one level is irrefutable. Important historical instances of masters who met this test include both 'Jigs-med Gling-pa and 'Jam-dbyangs mKhyen-brtse'i dBang-po, as well as their immediate incarnations.

Taking this way of thinking a step further, the titles we inherit may ultimately be less important than who we are and what we manifest. Not all tulkus are worthy of deep respect, and not all excellent lamas are tulkus. An incarnation lineage can be very helpful when the reborn lama has a particular role to fulfill (for instance, as the abbot of a monastery), but when that is not the case, perhaps the existence of the karmic connection from one incarnation to the next should not be a factor on which we place undue reliance.

For those of us who have been identified as tulkus, perhaps the best practice is for each of us to be our own witness, evaluating our own inner qualities and spiritual powers. For instance, how many past lives of spiritual endeavor can any of us truly recall? Based on that one test alone, how many of us would claim to be great Bodhisattvas or the highest of tulkus?

In my own case (and I am sure this holds true for others who hold the title tulku), I feel deeply connected to certain lamas of the past. How much of this feeling is psychological or the product of imagination, and how much reflects genuine memories, is hard to say. I certainly do not have the detailed memories of past lives that would allow me to claim the status of tulku with absolute confidence.

For this reason, I do not claim any special identity. It is true that I have had the rare opportunity to meet with great masters and to study at their feet, so some karmic connection must have existed. What I know for a fact is that throughout this life I have felt impelled to dedicate all my energies and merit to extend the teachings of the Buddha, and to do whatever I could to strengthen the Sangha. For me that is what matters.

In this respect, I do assign significance to my recognition as a tulku. As human beings, all of us have a duty to reflect on who we are and on how best to live this precious life. But those of us who bear the title tulku have a special responsibility to uphold it. We must take it upon ourselves to guarantee the truth of our inheritance, to determine how we can represent our lineage, and to further the transmission of the Dharma.

Dharma Study:
Purpose and Meaning

The Buddha taught that everything is open for investigation and inquiry: every belief, every scripture. There is no specific dogma, no truth that is beyond questioning and must be maintained. While Buddhism has conceptual content and doctrines, this content is open to challenge and inquiry. In fact, without such inquiry, the doctrines themselves will be of limited value in leading practitioners toward realization.

Still, the role of challenge and inquiry can easily be distorted. The ingrained patterns of thought and action that rule our minds cloud our ability to discern what will support us on the path. If we do not understand those patterns, the 'challenges' we mount will only reinforce our own positions, blocking access to the deeper meanings of the teaching. Until we learn to thoroughly investigate the mind, we do not have the resources to thoroughly investigate the teachings.

The potential for mind to operate with a wholesome clarity is available right now. If we do not have access to it, it is because this potential has been turned in a wrong direction or unwittingly obscured. The Dharma offers a path out of the fog of obscuration, but it is up to us to walk that path. This means determining for ourselves whether the fresh perspective that Dharma offers is grounded in true wisdom. It means not only refining our intellectual skills, but also allowing the aspiration for enlightenment to arise in our mind and take hold in our hearts. If this cannot be done, the foundation for an inquiry that challenges the workings of samsaric mind will not be established.

In Buddhism, 'right understanding' has nothing to do with accepting some particular set of beliefs or cultivating a faith not grounded in knowledge. The path is 'right' in the specific sense that it offers a fruitful way to learn, encouraging attitudes that will not interfere with the accumulation of insight. This is not a question of 'right' versus 'wrong'; it stems from the observation that the mind will recognize knowledge most readily when it is operating in wholesome ways that integrate all aspects of our being. In this sense, all forms of inquiry have therapeutic value, and free and open questioning is intrinsic to the path. This is not, however, an invitation to select aspects of Buddhism that one finds appealing while rejecting other aspects out of hand.

A questioning approach is well suited to the free-thinking Western intellectual tradition, for it sets no preconditions and accommodates any and all specific approaches. It fits especially well with the scientific disciplines, which emphasize the importance of direct and unbiased observation. If qualified Buddhist teachers are able to communicate these aspects of the Dharma to even a few individuals well-trained in Western knowledge traditions, Buddhism can make a lasting contribution to contemporary ways of thinking, and it will be possible to translate the wisdom of the Buddha into modern terms.

The essential first steps toward this transmission are now being taken. A growing number of individuals appreciate and respect the Dharma. Even if their study and practice have in some respects been haphazard and incomplete, their devotion reflects their understanding that the Dharma offers reliable knowledge and a wholesome way of being. As long as qualified and compassionate teachers continue to be available to guide them, sincerely motivated individuals can become good Dharma students capable of passing on the essence of the teachings to others. When this happens, the blessings of the Dharma are sure to manifest.

Nonetheless, the patterns of mind that operate in the contemporary world create substantial obstacles to Dharma transmission. Traditional teachers, accustomed to a very different culture, may not readily recognize these obstacles when they first manifest. In my own case, however, living and working closely with Westerners every day, I have learned to recognize the signs, and I have learned how deep-rooted such barriers to transmission can be.

Becoming a Dharma Student

The genuine openness and longing with which someone new to the Dharma may approach the teachings does not necessarily reflect a long-term dedication to study and practice. In particular, the beginning student's warmth and curiosity may not be matched by a willingness to proceed in accord with the traditional methods of training students in the Dharma. This gap between the student's initial enthusiasm and a whole-hearted commitment can be confusing to a teacher from a land with a strong history of Dharma transmission.

One source of difficulty is that new students may not realize how deep and complex the Dharma tradition of knowledge is. If this is so, they may be discouraged to discover that the path to realization requires patient study and practice and long-term dedication. If the student starts with unrealistic expectations, and the teacher fails to explain clearly what is involved, there is likely to be disappointment on both sides. Students who come to a teacher or a Dharma center with the idea that they will obtain tangible and immediate results will sooner or later grow disheartened. Even if they respect and appreciate the Dharma, they may eventually give up and leave. For a fledgling Dharma community, the impact of losing the very individuals who had seemed the most dedicated can be severe.

It is traditional in Buddhism to speak of one who follows the teachings as a student of the Dharma, but in some respects this can be misleading. It is not enough for a Dharma student to study the Dharma as a university student might study a major field, learning the intellectual content and then using that knowledge to pursue his or her specific interests. In Dharma studies no one ever graduates, at least not short of obtaining perfect enlightenment. The idea of becoming an authority on Dharma is foreign to the Buddhist tradition, and degrees or titles, while significant, do not have the same connotation of mastery that they do in the West. Study of the Dharma is not a matter of scholarship or proficiency, but rather a question of making one's life into Dharma activity, so that the path *is* one's life.

Again, in the Western academic tradition, the measure of progress is how well one performs on certain tests, or how well one can express or creatively apply what one has been taught. In Buddhism, on the other hand, the measure of success is how strongly spiritual qualities manifest in one's life. In part this means giving up any idea of personal benefit, including the idea of using what one has learned for one's own advantage.

The relation between student and teacher in the tradition is also very different from what Westerners might expect. In the West, it is natural for a student to want to 'get' something from the teacher, but in Tibet the student seeks to enter deeply into the teaching and embody it. This distinction has far-reaching consequences. For example, a Westerner would likely see nothing wrong in a student starting with one teacher and moving on to another at his or her own discretion. From a traditional perspective, however, when a student who has made a connection to a teacher feels the urge to seek out other teachers before the first teacher has acknowledged the completion of a certain level of training, it is a sign that samsaric mind—always ready to offer good reasons for breaking the discipline of practice—is in control. Following the wish to find the teacher one 'likes' best only reinforces old habits of mind, and seeking a style of teaching or practice that 'makes the most sense' to one's own way of thinking only puts off the essential task of investigating one's own most cherished mental patterns and presuppositions. True practice of the Dharma requires persistence and devotion powerful enough to overcome such predictable responses, which may well mean staying with a particular Dharma situation beyond the point where it feels comfortable. That is one reason the teacher/student relationship involves such heavy responsibilities on both sides, and why both teacher and student need to reflect carefully before committing themselves to it.

Of course, it is natural for practitioners who have turned to the Dharma to grow discouraged at times, and to wonder whether they are really making progress. Throughout the history of the Dharma even great masters have experienced doubt and considered giving up. Yet in the modern world, this tendency seems to be especially pronounced, and very often it leads people to break off their connection to the Dharma at a critical juncture.

Partly for this reason, I do not usually begin by giving students teachings that require total commitment. Instead, I invite them to participate in projects that contribute to the work of our centers in preserving and transmitting the Dharma. In this way, students have the opportunity to decide over time whether their interest is real. While they are busy with their work, they can engage different aspects of the teachings at their own pace, as their interest and appreciation grow. At the same time, they have the opportunity to take on greater commitments and responsibilities over time, which allows them to explore their own patterns and resistances at ever deeper levels. They can also see that their work here has practical benefits and results, which fits well with the pragmatic approach emphasized in the modern world. As they continue to practice in this way and their commitment to the Dharma grows, most eventually reach a point where it makes sense to begin the higher studies and practices that form part of the traditional course of instruction.

When a Dharma student is doing well, every moment becomes an opportunity for celebration and deepening appreciation. Studying the Dharma means falling in love with the Dharma—making the teachings a part of oneself and manifesting with ever greater intensity the qualities of enlightened knowledge. One useful measure for evaluating growth is to observe whether the student practices the Buddhist teachings on ethics and morality, for in the Dharma, virtue is the actualization of knowledge: a direct expression of one's understanding.

When appreciation for the teachings becomes strong and solid, the Dharma itself becomes the teacher. The individuals who help in this process can also be regarded as teachers, but the true student of the Dharma is one who makes a connection to the lineage and to the truth of what the Buddha taught. This link is more fundamental and more nourishing than any personal connection. The individual teacher who offers guidance and direction is more accurately regarded as a friend and counselor, able to assist the student in exploring the vast riches of the Dharma and to help prevent confusion or wrong views from arising.

Balancing Study and Practice

Until recently, few in the Western world knew anything of the Buddhist path. Now, as more and more individuals practice the Dharma, the realization is beginning to dawn that traveling the path requires a great deal of inner discipline, conscientious intelligence, mindfulness, and faithful study and practice.

All these qualities must be grounded in a comprehensive approach to the teachings, something that is not easy to obtain in our present state of knowledge. The Sūtrayāna, the path and practices based on the Sūtras, is vast, and the Mantrayāna, the path and practices based on the Tantric systems, is vaster still. Exploring their depths requires lifetimes of study, and transmitting their meaning accurately to the West will very likely require several generations.

Inquiry into the Dharma depends on cultivating a clear and balanced mind, which means learning to balance intellectual study and conceptual insight with meditative practice that opens new realms of experience. The knowledge that can be transmitted through words is certainly important. Without words to point out what has significance, we could never become aware of how samsaric mind perpetuates itself, nor could we conceive of ways to go beyond words. In this sense, intellect and language are indispensable tools for understanding the meaning of Dharma. Yet direct experience has a power that words cannot match. It allows us to discover and explore places within ourselves that no vocabulary is adequate to describe. Experiential inquiry teaches us that our thoughts, the vocabulary available to us, and our ordinary mind all have inherent limitations, and it gives us the means to break through those limitations.

When we are first developing our practice (and this stage may continue for many years), the discipline instilled through words and conceptual frameworks is an essential element in training the mind.

In learning to label and analyze experience, we begin to clear up certain confusions, making it possible for inner calm to develop. The activity of mind slows down and the kleśas, (emotional obscurations) fall silent. From this basis of inner calm, we can move into realms of knowledge in which conceptual structures have a very limited role to play. We find that we can investigate experience actively without losing our grounding in peaceful and balanced serenity. Through this interplay of tranquility and higher awareness (śamathā and vipaśyana), practice develops in a new way, making conceptual structures unnecessary.

Śamathā and vipaśyana are more than just tools that allow us to transform our practice. Their union represents the transformed state of mind that is the purpose of our practice. To enter this state is like entering a beautiful temple and discovering on the altar images of rare perfection. The outer layers of mind, dominated by obscurations, become still and clear, and meditative practice begins to reflect an entirely different way of operating the mind. We may make contact with an inner guide whose counsel is truly reliable.

As meditation deepens into new knowledge, the old obstacles that previously made up almost the whole of our inner reality are transformed. From the new perspective that begins to develop, there has never been a samsaric realm. Mind has the nature of Dharma (Dharmatā), and whatever exists proves inseparable from the truth of the Dharma and Sangha. Having learned how to embody that truth, we can trust in our experience and connect naturally to awakened wisdom.

Because the texts describe such states in beautiful and evocative ways, it is tempting to imagine that we can attain such realization immediately. But no matter how inspiring the descriptions, we cannot direct our practice in the right way if we do not first have some understanding of where we are headed. While Dharma students who value practice or devotion over 'intellectual' knowledge may not agree, my own view is that without the support of knowledge and understanding, it is difficult to bring practice to fulfillment. An intellectual grasp of the teachings is like the layer of muscles underneath the skin: It gives our practice inner strength.

Learning how to balance conceptual inquiry with a more direct appreciation for the truth of the Dharma comes through experience. In the beginning it is quite normal to emphasize one approach over the other, and up to a certain point this works well. But eventually we must find a point of balance for ourselves. This is why I consider basic studies in the Sūtra and śāstra traditions to be an essential background for the profound teachings of the Mantrayāna, gateway to such powerful realizations.

The balance between study and practice will be different for different individuals. For some it will be best to pursue their studies in monasteries or on retreat, or to work with more devotional practices. Those who respond to sacred art may find that its forms open doorways to understanding, while for others, work will prove most fruitful for challenging the positions of the self.

In our own community, we continue to experiment with the best ways to bring practice and conceptual inquiry to a point where they can merge, transforming both. At Odiyan, where I now live, this balance takes form on the basis of work dedicated to the Three Jewels. Most of the students who live and work within the Odiyan mandala have yet to develop a strong foundation in traditional Buddhist studies, but their work has given them the opportunity to benefit from the inspiration of knowledge.

Extraordinarily beautiful and isolated from the distractions and confusions of a world run by samsaric mind, Odiyan offers an environment and way of life that readily accommodate study and practice. Anyone who lives here has known times when space itself opens to meditative realization, when time gives permission for the old order to fall away, allowing new knowledge to enter. My hope is that in the future Odiyan will offer serious students a place where they can bring their lives into harmony with their practice, a center for study and practice that recreates the atmosphere traditionally considered most suited to following the path.

I do not mean to suggest that Dharma can be practiced only in a secluded setting such as Odiyan.

The teachings have far too much power to be confined in this way. Just as samsara is samsara, no matter how beautiful and inspiring one's surroundings, so the lineage of realization can manifest under any set of circumstances. For one firmly grounded in the Dharma, modern society offers constant instruction in the nature and origin of suffering. Those individuals who share most fully in the material benefits of our technologically advanced age are the ones most likely to have learned that even in the midst of plenty, lasting satisfaction cannot be found. Such knowledge is a strong ally, like being inoculated with a vaccination that offers protection against future suffering.

In much the same way, the widespread sense of confusion or uncertainty about how to live and what has value can be a strong support for study of the Dharma. A lack of knowledge about the purpose of being alive encourages an openness to new ideas and new teachings. For someone whose basic material wants are satisfied, the question may well arise: "Is this the way I want to spend the rest of my life?" Asked honestly, this question generates a momentum of inquiry. Pursued to its fullest, the path of questioning leads naturally to the Dharma, the one true alternative to the destructive patterns of samsara and the pain they bring.

If we can learn to approach the complex patterns of contemporary society with an open, inquiring spirit, engaging the structures of mind we discover at work in playful and creative ways, life in the city can be at least as interesting and fruitful for Dharma practice as a life lived in retreat from the world. Still, it is no easy task to maintain a meditative equanimity within an urban lifestyle. For most people a retreat environment similar to Odiyan's will provide a more stable foundation for exploring the teachings of the Buddha in depth and practicing in ways that integrate study and meditation.

The Importance of Study

Academic study in modern society tends to be highly specialized and exclusively intellectual in its orientation. Perhaps for this reason, some Dharma students dismiss the value of seeking an intellectual understanding of the teachings. Yet my own view is different. Properly applied, conceptual knowledge can be the solid foundation for practice. It dispels many kinds of confusion, opens up a broader perspective on the teachings, and counteracts the tendency to believe that familiarity with one particular area of Buddhist thought makes one a master of the entire Buddhist tradition. For anyone who wishes to create more accurate translations or educate others in the meaning and significance of the Buddha's teachings, academic study is essential. Only through this kind of knowledge can the Buddha's wisdom be made available to people in the modern world.

For serious Dharma students, the śāstra tradition transmitted from India to Tibet, together with works by Tibetan masters on the topics that the śāstras introduce, offer a particularly rich resource for study and for knowledge of the Dharma: a body of wisdom that remains alive and vigorous today. These teachings explore the meaning of human existence, the valid means of knowledge, and the best way to live one's life—questions common to all great thinkers. Abhidharma offers highly effective methods for a careful investigation of experience and the nature of reality, while the works of the Mādhyamika school introduce powerful methods of analysis, a precise and illuminating vocabulary, and tools for logic and epistemology that develop sharp and clear perception. In some cases, issues and difficulties that have come to light in the West only in the past few centuries have been the subject of inquiry in Buddhism for more than two thousand years.

The power of the Dharma tradition never ceases to amaze me. Just to read a few lines by such great masters as Klong-chen-pa, 'Jigs-med Gling-pa, 'Jam-dbyangs mKhyen-brtse dBang-po, dPal-sprul Rinpoche, or Lama Mi-pham is to discover hidden places in consciousness more wonderful than any paradise. The insights that their teachings communicate to our ordinary minds, so enmeshed in daily concerns and misunderstandings, are a treasure of inconceivable worth.

As a young man in Tibet, I knew many lamas who dedicated years of their lives to studying such remarkable works. I remember how they would pore over these texts, focusing all their attention for hours on end. Study in that context had nothing to do with passing examinations, obtaining a degree, or being hired for a position. It grew out of their intense involvement with questions raised by the Dharma, which inspired such one-pointed devotion that they seemed to regard even eating and sleeping as time taken away from what had real value.

Today the changing circumstances that history has forced upon us have put severe limits on this kind of intense engagement with the teachings. Certainly the course of my own life has not left me with much time for study. Yet I know enough of the tradition to be able to say with certainty that the West would benefit greatly from having these works more widely available. My impression is that the Yogācāra and Cittamātra teachings, introduced to the West through China and Japan, also hold special interest for the modern world. Buddhist logic (pramāṇa) is another important field to engage, for by studying logic it is possible to learn how meaning is constructed: a little like studying the engineering that goes into building a great bridge.

In Tibet, five traditional śāstra topics were studied by all the schools: Vinaya, Abhidharma, Prajñā-pāramitā, Madhyamaka, and Pramāṇa. Since each of these topics usually requires several years of full-time study, true mastery comes only after a dozen years or more of intensive study and practice. One might spend many years engaged in the in-depth study of just a few key texts, relating them to different themes and topics and comparing different interpretations. In the Nyingma tradition, thirteen texts from the śāstra tradition of India were considered especially important for everyone to know. Not all of them are available in translation, but those that are would be an excellent point of departure. While students raised in a country without a strong Dharma tradition will face certain handicaps in penetrating to the core of these teachings, I am sure that anyone willing to devote twenty or thirty years to careful investigation of these texts will attain profound levels of understanding. Following such a course may transform the understanding of knowledge itself, inviting a fundamental rethinking of present models of thought and education that can have a major impact on society at large.

At present there may not be many people who are able to appreciate the full depths of such teachings. I myself lack the training and insight that would enable me to do so. But we can still hope that some day this understanding will flourish once again. If an epidemic can spread the evils of disease and death, why can there not be an epidemic of realization: a cycle of awakening that gathers momentum until it rolls ahead with the thundering roar of an ocean wave—the lion's roar of realization, transcending all ordinary knowledge and all obstacles? Why cannot knowledge create itself, instantly, like a fire that flares up spontaneously, leaving no possibility of mistake?

Conceptual Insight and Awareness

Many Dharma students whose backgrounds and interests clearly suggest that they would benefit from serious study of the traditional teachings dismiss the ultimate importance of such study. When I ask them why, they tell me they consider it more important to master the higher teachings, such as rDzogs-chen. But I consider this a false distinction. Once a lama friend of mine, a true practitioner of rDzogs-chen, said to me that anyone who understood the Madhyamaka way of self-analysis could comprehend rDzogs-chen with very little effort. At the time I was surprised that a rDzogs-chen master would say this, but today I think I know what he meant. The Madhyamaka understanding of śūnyatā clarifies the nature of mind, providing a solid foundation for rDzogs-chen practice.

When practice is rooted in śūnyatā, appearance and emptiness are seen as inseparable. In that case—when everything appears as openness—is it even possible to fall from realization back into samsara? When there is no place to fall, what can be false? There can be no faults and also no being fooled. The body itself becomes the sky, and the lion's roar, the vastness sound of realization, transmits itself effortlessly in all directions.

The special power of rDzogs-chen is to make such realization, identical to that obtained by the Buddha through endless kalpas of effort, available in this life-time. Yet the foundation of rDzogs-chen, the starting point and also the bottom line, is the study of śūn-yatā. The practitioner starts with conceptual inquiry, never resting until knowledge becomes pervasive and obstacles are transformed into the two accumulations of merit and wisdom. This activates a momentum that leads to full understanding of the nature of mind, and the emotionality and wrong views that sustain samsara no longer arise.

Those who doubt that the ordinary mind can arrive at ultimate knowledge will have a hard time using analysis to gain access to deeper understanding. But the distinction between ordinary and ultimate is itself an impediment. For those who are open-minded, study and practice build on one another. The teachings point the way toward deeper practice, and as practice deepens, we ourselves, in our own embodiment, *become* the teachings.

It is true that conceptual inquiry depends on the structures of ordinary mind, but if those structures are themselves not solid, why should this be a restriction? The scriptures teach that enlightenment is possible only because we are already inseparable from the potential for enlightenment, like muddy water that is by nature clear. In that case, why reject what the mind has to offer? Why let our own critical judgments or reactions to conceptual inquiry have the final word?

The Dharma offers a special way to exercise our intellect. The point is not to compile a dictionary of meanings that allows us to accept or reject, but to ask how the mind reacts with judgments and labels functions. Where do meanings come from? How do perception and experience come into being? How do they come alive? How is experience set up and clothed in its identity?

Pursuing such questions, we may be tempted to engage in lengthy stories with complicated plots. While stories can seem immensely interesting, it can be even more interesting to investigate what makes 'interesting' interesting. Perhaps in the end, when we realize that the stories we tell are only variations on stories that everyone has been telling since time immemorial, we will decide that the interesting is not really interesting after all. Interesting in itself, that realization provides us incisive information about existence in the world and raises fundamental questions about who we are. How is it that matters have gone on in this same way for so long? If patterns repeat themselves, what does it mean to have a new thought? Do all thoughts take place within a circumscribed horizon, or can the horizon for thinking itself change?

By questioning mind and its activity, we learn to make good use of both our bodies and our minds. The more we ask, the more we are able to direct our intelligence and our actions differently: to move more readily toward what has meaning. The way we see, the way we think, the way we make sense of reality on the relative level: All such structures become available for restructuring. Whoever we are, whatever our training or status, this is knowledge we can draw on to give significance to our lives. In this way, intellectual inquiry opens a rich new way of being, one we can embody directly.

The path toward such realization—the path of study and reflection—is not difficult to engage. Thinking and questioning have their own dynamic. When we look toward our thoughts—not to focus on their contents, label their presentations, or count their appearings, but to appreciate their character and presence as thoughts—we are already embodying this dynamic.

When we learn to cultivate insight through the traditional three-stage path of study, reflection on what we have studied, and practice, we see for ourselves the value of a balanced approach to knowledge. Eventually we realize that the enlightened qualities are available to us. We discover that our own availability for knowledge is the availability of the teachings to be known—that we are partners with the Buddhas. Then practice becomes easy.

When study and inquiry come fully into play, they give substance and form to our practice. Knowledge opens naturally, like the petals of a blossom that turns toward the sun. The ordinary and immediately present reality of our own existence becomes the foundation for the most esoteric knowledge. We discover that relative and ultimate truth reflect an underlying unity, a coexistence that cannot be readily expressed, but is readily available.

To separate them *is* relative truth, while to see their interpenetration is to arrive at the ultimate perspective. At this 'ultimate' level, study can indeed come to an end. There is no longer any point in talking about truth, or in giving any account at all. There is no basis for comparison and nothing left to say.

How Can the Dharma
Benefit Our Lives Today?

*O*n the late 1960s, when I arrived in the West, there was an openness to new ideas and lifestyles that favored receptivity to certain aspects of the Buddhist teachings. While interest in the Dharma has grown substantially since then, the nature of this interest has changed. Today spiritual values are increasingly overshadowed by the lure of materialism, a growing concern for security, professionally fulfilling careers, and the fascinations of technology. Those who seek out the Dharma today are more likely to ask how the teachings of the Buddha can be applied—in science, in psychology, in work, or in dealing with such common concerns as stress and tension.

This secular and down-to-earth approach to Buddhism can be very valuable, but it does create certain obstacles to deepening spiritual practice. The difficulty is not that a secular outlook is opposed to religion, but rather that too great a concern with material values consumes time and mental energy, allowing few opportunities for pondering questions on the meaning and significance of life. If such questions cease to matter, not only religion, but also philosophy and psychology as well as many other fields of knowledge and inquiry, will soon begin to seem irrelevant.

Buddhism may actually help heal this potential split between secular concerns and spiritual or existential inquiry. In the tradition of Dharma, the focus on how the teachings can be applied has always been central. The aim of following the path is not to arrive at some kind of theoretical understanding of the human condition, but to release human beings from the burden of karmic obligations and free the mind from its self-imposed limitations. According to the Dharma, knowledge must serve the whole range of human needs and concerns, both secular and religious. In fact, secular and religious concerns and values must unite for the true meaning of the Dharma to be realized.

Sometimes critics charge that those individuals who are drawn to the Dharma are unable to deal with the realities of life and are looking for an easy way to escape conventional responsibilities. But as soon as the connection between daily concerns and the teachings of the Buddha becomes clear, this charge makes little sense. Nor does it accord with the reality of practicing the Dharma, for it is hard to imagine a more demanding calling—intellectually, ethically, or in terms of taking responsibility on a daily basis.

In many ways, the secular values and orientation of the West support the practice of the Dharma. On a basic level, the principle of religious freedom means that students of Buddhism can pursue their own path without interference. In practical terms, the advances in communication in modern society, coupled with ideals of individual freedom and equality of opportunity, give nearly everyone easy access to information about Buddhism. Finally, the West strongly supports education and knowledge, both of which are fundamental Buddhist values, even if it understands those concepts very differently than in the Buddhist tradition.

On a more subtle level, several trends in the modern world foster an appreciation for essential elements in the teachings. The countless changes brought by technology, the emphasis on innovation, and the endless stream of information and entertainments all support the realization that there are many different ways to use the mind and numerous forms of knowledge. After all, we live in a society where knowledge has completely transformed our lives. Since this transformation is ongoing, the power of the mind is always visible right before our eyes, affecting us subliminally if not overtly.

Today, when individuals from all walks of life realize that knowledge can come from unexpected sources, the potential value of the Dharma can readily be acknowledged and appreciated. This interest in turn can help promote the availability and transmission of the teachings. If circumstances come together in the right way—in Buddhist terms, if the karma is ripe—realization may not be that difficult to obtain or to transmit to others.

Linking Traditional Buddhism with Modern Thought

The Buddha taught that the answer to our difficulties is found within the mind, and this message fits well with present ways of thinking. In a society where new technologies routinely uproot established customs, and where cultural influences from around the world steadily interact, the central role of the mind in shaping experience is almost self-evident. Though we may be accustomed to using the mind in routine ways, it is natural to acknowledge that the mind contains hidden depths. On some level, it seems easy for people to imagine that an exploration of those depths could open a path that leads all the way to enlightenment.

Present social and intellectual trends support an openness to the Dharma at another level. There is a growing recognition that the type of knowledge cultivated for the last several centuries in the West, marvelous as it is, is also suffused with a kind of toxicity that has caused untold harm. Today we seem bound to samsara more tightly than ever. We could say that samsara has become our only refuge, which is just another way of saying that we have no refuge at all. Recognizing the harmful consequences of this way of life, many individuals have searched for some alternative. Even if this kind of inquiry does not lead them to withdraw from the world to become monks and nuns, it does make it easier to recognize how deeply trapped we have become in confusion and not-knowing, and how often the problems that we face are self-generated.

The issue could be put in this way: The materialistic values that modern society serves and stimulates aim at fulfilling the desires of the self. Yet we seem unable to attain this goal, at least if we judge in terms of fulfillment or lasting satisfaction. Then could there be a way to satisfy the self's desires that works—one that gives new meaning and fulfillment to our lives? The Dharma offers one possible answer, but it should not be understood as telling us simply to put an end to desire and pleasure and live our lives on some other basis. The teachings of the Buddha invite us to stop taking the desiring mind for granted, and to ask instead how it is that desire arises. It teaches us to cultivate knowledge of mind, so that we can deal with desire on a new basis.

Mind is deeply variable. It can sink into dullness, waste our time with trivialities, or manufacture stories that hide the truth of our condition, but it can also be deeply creative, giving birth to what is truly joyful and meaningful. Once we accept that both these alternatives are equally available—that mind as it is right now can fulfill mind—we realize that the secular mind can move beyond its own limits. The door is open to a peace more profound than the sated feeling of satisfied desire, and a security more certain than that which comes with ownership.

The issue of linking the Dharma to present-day values and pursuits seems to me of fundamental importance. The books I have written in the Nyingma Psychology Series, though nothing more than simple introductions to certain Buddhist themes and topics, are one way in which I have tried to make such connections. Similarly, the books in the Time, Space, and Knowledge Series (TSK) promote a style of inquiry that is well-suited to Dharma study and secular concerns alike. For certain individuals, including intellectuals and scientists highly skeptical toward all religions, these works, which make no dogmatic claims and establish no belief systems, may serve as a point of entry to a knowledge that goes beyond the ordinary mind.

The TSK vision could be seen as a response to a dynamic unique to this culture. As a secular way of thinking increasingly calls into question the belief systems that once governed this society, there have been two major responses. One response (prevalent in certain religious groups) is to withdraw from contact with those outside the circle of believers. But there are also those thinkers and practitioners who attempt to bring their own beliefs into harmony with the views and beliefs of the society they inhabit. On the one hand, the dividing lines or edges between competing sets of beliefs become more sharply defined; on the other hand, more and more people move into the great open spaces between these narrow enclaves, attempting to shape beliefs and values that could be considered universal.

TSK could be seen as a teaching for these open spaces. It insists on no moral principles, founds no temples, initiates no priests, and relies on nothing remotely resembling prayer or worship. However, the openness that shapes TSK operates in a different dimension. TSK rejects the dichotomy between 'open' and 'closed' and the separation of 'inside' from 'outside.' From a TSK perspective, beliefs do not emerge to shape reality from some inaccessible, privileged place. Knowledge is already available, free to present itself by taking any form whatsoever.

For those who might otherwise be wary of any claims to 'higher' knowledge, this approach effectively dissipates such concerns, suggesting that we could replace knowledge 'of', in all its competing flavors, with a more global knowledge 'in'. And it locates the source of this new knowledge not somewhere else, but in a playful questioning of the knowledge upon which we already rely. In practical terms, this means that individuals are not bound to any hierarchy. They can adopt with equal facility the role of teacher or student, observer or participant.

Independence from Authority

Despite the many ways in which the teachings of Buddhism are consistent with a secular orientation, there are also potential points of conflict. One of the most important is the tendency among those who grow up in a secular culture to reject all forms of authority. Students of Buddhism, whether they have been brought up in an agnostic or atheistic household or have turned away from the belief system of the religion they were raised in, often exhibit this anti-authoritarian streak. In consequence, they tend to maintain that they should be free to develop their own understanding of Buddhism, even where it conflicts with the tradition. I have reflected extensively on this issue, but here I want to consider it specifically in terms of the claim to personal autonomy: the right of each individual to find his or her own way, rather than simply following what others have done or believed in the past.

There is something deeply right in this way of thinking, which brings the practice of open inquiry to the fore. Yet it is also possible for individuals who insist on following their own belief systems and personal set of values to cut off the spirit of inquiry just at the point where the Dharma suggests they should most vigorously exercise it. For although they challenge all revealed values and truths, they forget to challenge the one who is challenging. No inquiry into mind from a Buddhist perspective can afford to leave unexamined so central an element in our experience. Perhaps it will be helpful to sketch out in detail how such an examination might proceed.

The difficulty with insisting that each individual should be free to decide what has value and what should be followed is that it enshrines the motivations of the self. In effect, this means making the individual's beliefs immune to inquiry. The right to 'independent' inquiry becomes the right to depend on 'my' self: my motives and convictions, beliefs and presuppositions. But where do these come from? Are they simply an expression of my likes and dislikes? If so, can I trace the source of such emotional reactions, or must I simply conclude that 'being independent' ultimately means acting arbitrarily, for no particular reason except that it is 'my' way?

When I choose to act on the basis of personal convictions and values, I seem to be saying that I am attached to my own way of thinking and feeling. But why should I believe that my own thoughts and preferences are any more 'true' or reliable than those of others? Why should I agree to depend on this source for guidance? In taking this stand, have I not become a follower at a different level?

The claim that the self should be the one to choose its own way seems to be based in part on a split that I create between self as actor and self as the source of values. But who is this 'I' that holds and imposes beliefs, if not the actor? When I turn myself into the authority I rely on, is this separate self real at all?

Again, is the knowledge proclaimed by a self more trustworthy than any other? If not, the decisions I make on the basis of that knowledge may well be the wrong decisions. Provided I care whether my decisions are right or wrong, whether they have value for myself and others, this seems an unacceptable outcome. Perhaps I choose to follow 'my' view because I am convinced that ultimately no source of knowledge is reliable. But in that case, my mind is already closed to the fundamental teaching of the Dharma that a higher or deeper knowledge is available to each of us. Can we really build a new version of Buddhism on such a problematic basis?

There may be a way to rethink the issue of autonomy that offers an alternative to these dead-end options. When we rely on ourselves as the source of knowledge, we are agreeing to take responsibility for that knowledge, which is invariably 'mine'. In that case, 'I' have an obligation to question 'my' knowledge as thoroughly as possible. How do we know that our views are right or reliable? How could we investigate to make sure this was so? Is it enough that we can give reasons for our actions, or do we need to develop some more trustworthy kind of knowledge, based on a deeper understanding of how 'my' mind operates? Do we know how to begin this kind of inquiry?

Theoretically, we might insist on autonomy but reject responsibility for our own knowledge and actions. In that case, we are saying that we can do whatever we want, without justifying it to ourselves or anyone else. Perhaps we are led to such a claim in the name of personal freedom and equality. Yet what if our choices lead toward the destruction of freedom, for ourselves and for others? Can we just accept that possibility, relying on the fact that this is not our intention? What if further inquiry, not grounded in 'my' convictions at all, could reveal that this is where our course of conduct is headed? Could we refuse to engage it?

We might argue in response that knowledge can never get past the self and its motives, or claim that a more reliable knowledge is unavailable. We have seen already that such a claim seems to go against the fundamental teachings of the Buddha. But it also goes against the way we function in the world. Often we do demand a knowledge more reliable than our own unsupported convictions: That is why we have doctors and pilots, for example. Why adopt a different rule when it comes to governing our lives, especially when doing so leads us into difficulties again and again? Why give special privileges to our knowledge and make it unquestionable?

If we do decide, despite all this, that the desires and motivations of the self are beyond questioning or justification, we may have given away more than we think. The Buddhist analysis of mind suggests that our way of manifesting as a self cannot be separated from the other ways in which we know. For example, the self-image is interwoven with the senses: It is as a self that we see and hear, and if our sense of self changed, what we saw and heard would change as well. In the same way, what we regard as rational or fair will reflect the order and values that the self-image sets up. Thus, if we exempt the self from inquiry, we are likewise exempting from inquiry the world as it appears to our senses and the set of values we evoke as just or worthy. What is left? What has become of the commitment to inquiry that underlies the practice of Dharma?

To rely on the self as ultimate arbiter is to restrict the realm of the questionable to those areas that are of no real significance for the self. Seeing in one way only, I have no basis for taking an independent stand. Choosing one particular course of action, I close off access to the place in my guts that might say, "Look again!" By insisting on the autonomy of the self, by guaranteeing that the son will always be loyal to the father, we do more (or less) than free ourselves from authority. We affirm the reign of ignorance.

A New Source of Knowledge

In rejecting authority in the name of the self, we seem to deliver ourselves over to the most tyrannical authority of all. Rather than looking for reliable knowledge, we settle for what 'I' want, for no more persuasive reason than that 'I' say so. We set up our own hierarchy, our own 'Church of the Self'. Even if we suspect that the decision-maker has no special claim to knowledge, the structure has already been established. The perception is complete, the identification absolute. It is futile to resist.

Suppose we tried to circumvent the rule of a tyrannical self by acting with absolute spontaneity. The difficulty with this approach is that the perceptions that guide even the most spontaneous action are shaped in advance by the regime of the self. After all, unless I rely on the roll of the dice, what possible basis can there be for the self's 'spontaneous' actions, if not the self's likes and dislikes? If we rely on likes and dislikes, our choice is not spontaneous after all, for like and dislike also come into being on the basis of the self's previous experience. In the end, proclaiming the autonomy of the self substitutes "I want" for "I know." Such claims to independence turn out to be the clothes the self wears to cover its naked desire.

If there is any justification for holding to the self as absolute authority, it comes in response to the idea that no one else should have power over us. But this approach gives away too much to the imagined oppressor, for it makes power, rather than knowledge, the final judge. It is hard to imagine a position more contrary to the teachings of the Dharma.

All this may sound exaggerated, but my experience in this country has convinced me otherwise. The idea of personal autonomy is so deeply rooted in Western Dharma students that they play out its consequences with very little self-awareness. One day a student serves the Dharma, because that is his wish; the next day he abandons his service, because that has become his wish. The self as arbitrary master is the shadow dogging the footsteps of each meritorious act.

Depending on such a master, we live a life in which everything is uncertain and ungrounded. We cannot say with conviction that we will consistently act on our highest values, nor can we count on making a maximum effort to develop a mind that is stable and focused. Yet without that stability, there is no way to develop the power of contemplation or pursue knowledge effectively. When the mind splits in different directions, we live with a steady sense of conflict. Heart and head fall out of balance, and we find ourselves unable to generate the dynamic that can cut through the snares samsara sets for us.

The Dharma teaches a different way. Human knowledge does not have to be referred automatically to the authority of the self. Without taking on issues of ownership and autonomy, we can simply resolve to train ourselves toward more knowledge and greater awareness. We can learn to hear and observe and analyze the circumstances in which we find ourselves. Before we act, before we accept the claims of the self, we have the opportunity to question what we are doing and to ask ourselves at a deeper level what knowledge guides our action. Even a little opening is enough to begin. Gradually we can educate ourselves and establish a more secure basis for what we do.

This possibility is available at any moment. As we try to make sense of our lives in a more cohesive way, we can look at the stories we tell. We can evaluate our actions to see when we have been successful and when we have failed, recognizing the recurring patterns of positive/negative and up/down. We can ask what knowledge generally informs our decisions and consider how to make our decisions more reliable. Instead of turning automatically to 'I', 'mine', and 'self', we can develop a more balanced approach to living that is free from all forms of authority. When we step off the roller-coaster ride of self-image, inquiry into knowledge can become a part of our work, our study, our practice, and our being. We can develop stability and invite the teachings to transform our hearts and minds.

If Westerners can learn to relax the strong focus on personal autonomy, the Dharma offers a path based on knowing who we are and how we function. Once this is seen, matters become relatively simple. If we study and practice the Dharma directly, without too much concern about whether we are yielding control to a teacher or to a tradition rooted in different historical circumstances, we can also study the self, and this is the most vital study of all. Studying the self, we begin to understand what we are doing and why. We discover the clarity and resolve to cut through the excuses and justifications we use to deceive ourselves and others. The voice of the Dharma makes itself heard in our hearts, bringing its message of joy and insight.

For a Dharma student who has reached this kind of understanding, questions about being in the right place or doing the right thing, issues of authority and autonomy, melt away. Whether studying, working, meditating, or looking out for the welfare of others, there is no need to chase after something we do not have, or to go somewhere else. For such a student, it is increasingly natural to focus on projects that serve the Dharma, and the religious and devotional aspects of the Dharma seem increasingly appropriate. Understanding based on direct experience vibrates through the heart and head and gut, and the goal toward which we are all working becomes increasingly clear.

Embodying the Teachings

Until we embody the Dharma, our relation to the teachings will be distanced and not completely satisfying in all ways. Although we may study with deep appreciation, ultimately we can only guess at the meaning of the texts we admire and rely on.

The way to embody the teachings is to enter the tradition. Some students might wish it could be otherwise, so we could stand on our own and leap directly into the heart of realization. But if that is the course we choose to enact, we run a very real risk that we are merely replicating (and passing on to others) our own ignorance and confusion.

Entering the tradition means giving up the insistence that Buddhism conform to the ways of understanding allowed by ordinary mind and conventional knowledge. It means turning instead to the in-depth study and practice of the scriptures and commentaries written over so many centuries of the Buddhist tradition, and having the patience to allow that study and practice to bear fruit.

Until that point is reached, it seems better for individuals practicing the Dharma not to comment too extensively on the tradition or the teachings, even when they are motivated by deep regard for the value of the teachings and appreciate the role of the lineages in their transmission. For if the mind is still deluded, how can it know its own nature? And if it does not know its own nature, how can it judge experience or convey the inner meaning of the Dharma? If 'rational' mind, with its host of judgments, is committed to perpetuating its own conditioning, how can it claim the right to accept or reject other forms of knowing? How can it apply its own values and standards to a different form of understanding?

Ordinary, 'rational' mind works by evaluating an object of perception, whether it be a physical object, a person, or an abstraction. Turning outward toward the object of attention, it turns away from understanding the subject, the one who is making the judgments or developing the understanding. The Dharma, however, tells us that until we understand the subject well, we have no access to reliable knowledge. Prajñā, the highest wisdom, is inseparable from knowledge of the mind that knows; indeed, it is the embodiment of such knowledge. When prajñā is operating, its clarity illuminates all that the mind sees; when it is absent or ignored, the mind manifests only delusion.

Underlying this distinction is a very real difficulty. If knowledge depends on mind, and mind investigates knowledge, how can we ever test the accuracy of our knowledge or rely on the judgments that mind makes? The traditional image used to illustrate this problem is a person suffering from jaundice, for whom everything in the world is tinged with yellow. When mind is the organ of perception, we perceive only what the mind is capable of perceiving, and we interpret it only in ways the mind finds reliable and trustworthy. And if the mind is mistaken in its views or faulty in its operations, we will have no way to know.

The best answer to this dilemma is to study the way the mind works. The Sūtras, the Abhidharma teachings, and the śāstra tradition teach us about mind and explore in depth the kinds of mental events that arise in our stream of consciousness: how they operate and interact. With such knowledge, we can learn to see how we fall into delusion and mistaken views. The more deeply we go into such studies and practice in accord with their teachings, the more we learn about the right view taught by the Buddha, and the closer we come to understanding the meaning of Dharma. As this knowledge settles into our being, mind itself is transformed.

It may be difficult to make sense of such a statement, for today, perhaps more than in other times
in history, we seem to be convinced that there is
only one way for the mind to work (at least when it
is working well). Even if we acknowledge the possibility of enlightened mind, it is a concept too remote
from us to be meaningful. Yet that is not what the
Buddha taught. The Dharma tells us that mind can
indeed operate differently, and it offers the means
for bringing this about.

These teachings and this way of proceeding are
not esoteric. They are already encompassed in the
Noble Eightfold Path, which the Buddha revealed in
the course of his first teaching at the Deer Park in
Sārnāth. But the fact that these teachings are fundamental and basic does not mean that we can
afford to brush past them as though they were
somehow too simple and obvious to bother with. It
is just this very knowledge that breaks through the
patterns of samsaric mind and allows us to turn
away from samsara and toward the Dharma.

As we learn to attune body, speech, and mind to
the Dharma through patience, honesty, and disciplined inquiry, knowledge will unfold into new
realms, far beyond what we presently think is possible. Even though we are still caught by ordinary
mind, our realization that this mind and its ways of
operating are deceptive allow us to gain clarity and
order within samsara. This is the foundation for all
realization. It is the way to embody the path.

In one sense, this way of understanding is not easily developed or sustained. Yet no matter where we are on the path, we can foster deeper appreciation and encourage the growth of insight. The way to do this is to study and practice in an orderly way the entire range of the Buddha's teachings, known in the Nyingma tradition as the Nine Vehicles or Yānas. By deliberately cultivating a vision of the whole, we come to understand how the universal truths of the Dharma can be expressed in different ways and for different purposes, meeting the needs of different individuals—all without distorting the Buddha's teachings.

We can begin right now to deepen our connection to the Dharma. If we open our eyes to the truth inherent within our own experience and open our hearts to the value of the teachings that the Buddha made available, the lineage of realization can manifest—so simply and directly that it becomes almost tangible. We should never forget how fortunate we are to have ready access to Dharma materials and to be blessed with the opportunity to live in circumstances that promote concentrated study, work, and practice. From a Dharma perspective, to have all these supports is a dream come true.

For those who live and work in the Nyingma community, these prerequisites are all in place. The essential Dharma teachings are available and the environment that supports study and practice—the outer forms and symbols of the mandala of realization—has been created over the course of thirty years. Now that those forms exist, we need only engage them fully and let their meaning manifest in our hearts. It is only our own conditioned views and attitudes that prevent us from learning to enact the Dharma and contact true enlightened knowledge.

In this very moment, we can let the blessings of Padmasambhava enter our hearts and nourish ourselves with our own feelings of appreciation. We can visualize the Sangha of the Enlightened Ones, reflect on the meaning of the Dharma, or silently chant mantras. As our life becomes richer and more productive through a stronger heart-connection with the Dharma, we can participate with greater creativity in the unfolding of our destiny.

The more we learn to follow this path, the more we embody the Dharma. Our studies take on new meaning and our lives become the unfolding of the teachings. Every day is a wonderful journey, and every new opportunity to read and reflect on the Dharma brings new richness into our experience. The knowledge we gain lets us master whatever projects we undertake and gives us the resources to overcome each new obstacle. Our creations become our path: skillful means for deepening understanding, for our own sake and for the sake of all beings. As knowledge itself expands, we realize that we are *inside* knowledge: inseparable from the symbols we have created and the wisdom they express.

Academic Approaches
to the Dharma

For more than a century, Buddhism has been a subject of study for Western academics. For much of this time, it has been treated as something dead and distant, as a historian might treat the texts and accounts of some long vanished civilization. But this is no longer always the case for the new generation of academics. Many younger scholars are drawn to the study of Buddhism out of personal interest in the teachings, and they share a conviction that the knowledge passed down in the Buddhist tradition has value for contemporary culture. Some of my own students have pursued an academic career for just such reasons.

The personal involvement of younger scholars in Dharma practice is certainly a helpful development. When academics start from the premise that the Dharma has value for Western society, they ask different kinds of questions, conduct different kinds of research, and read the texts in a more receptive way.

Nonetheless, the academic approach to Dharma differs in fundamental ways from the attitude and methods of inquiry that a Dharma student would traditionally adopt. Dharma practitioners who also operate in the academic world are often critical of certain aspects of the Dharma. They may question the authenticity of certain texts or practices that they do not consider to represent the Dharma accurately, and they are likely to adopt Western methods of resolving historical issues that contradict traditional approaches.

These conflicts and contradictions can be confusing for Dharma students who are following a more traditional path of inquiry and practice. The authority of the academic approach is well ingrained among Dharma students with a university education, and there is a tendency to assume that a scholar who is also sympathetic toward the Dharma is a reliable source of information about the Dharma, even where that scholar takes stands that undermine the tradition in various ways. Students concerned about these issues have often asked for my opinion. How can Western academic approaches be reconciled with the tradition? Is it worthwhile to make the attempt?

Sources of Conflict

My own impression is that Dharma students who attempt to make a home for themselves in the scholarly world are choosing a difficult path. Almost inevitably, they will encounter serious obstacles in reconciling their academic training and approach with the path to understanding as it is taught in the tradition. This can cause confusion on the personal level. From a Dharma perspective, when academic priorities gain the upper hand, the consequences can be deeply unfortunate.

The academic who is also a Dharma student will generally be under pressure to adopt a critical, disengaged stance toward his or her subject matter. Even though this attitude makes no sense at all within a living Dharma tradition, in an academic setting the issue is hardly open to debate. The moment a scholar declares his or her commitment to the practice of Dharma, colleagues begin to harbor doubts about that scholar's ability to be 'objective'. If the scholar goes on to demonstrate a willingness to accept the authority of the traditional accounts and interpretations at face value, there is almost no possibility for maintaining academic credibility or developing a successful academic career.

One option for the scholar sympathetic to Buddhism is to work out a personal understanding of what counts as 'real' or 'essential' Dharma. This approach allows for maintaining an attitude of respect and appreciation for some of the teachings, while not transgressing the boundaries of academic orthodoxy. It enables the Dharma student to lay claim to that elusive 'objectivity' on which colleagues are certain to insist.

The difficulty with this approach is that academic standards of 'objectivity' depend completely on modern Western notions of what counts as historical fact, what is possible for human beings, and what sources of knowledge are to be accepted as valid. Once such standards are adopted, whole chapters of traditional Buddhism prove to be in need of reinterpretation or 'demythologizing'.

For example, an academically trained scholar will 'date' a Sūtra or Tantra hundreds of years after the Buddha's parinirvāṇa, thus effectively stating it is not the Buddha's teaching, and will dismiss out of hand the traditional notion that a text may derive through a Sambhogakāya lineage not bound to the usual historical framework. Another example, from the field of Nyingma studies, is the academic preoccupation with tracing the 'source' of rDzogs-chen teachings. Scholars have variously argued that rDzogs-chen is really a Bon-po sect, a Hva-shang (Ch'an) teaching, a form of Kashmiri Śaivism, or a variant of Sufism.

In propounding such claims, scholars usually fail to acknowledge that Western knowledge in these areas is in the preliminary stages, and that it is easy to arrive at mistaken impressions when knowledge is incomplete. Such ideas and theories inevitably undermine the authority of the tradition. As to whether they advance the growth of wisdom and compassion, the question is simply irrelevant in an academic context, where all that matters is the truth—as truth is determined by contemporary evidentiary standards.

As long as such distanced styles of inquiry dominate, certain aspects of the Dharma will remain inaccessible to scholarly inquiry. For example, it is difficult to fully comprehend the enlightened qualities of the Buddha until one has perfected yogic modes of perception. But the scholar whose training is academic rather than yogic will not even treat seriously the possibility of taking such an approach.

Given these preconditions, it is virtually impossible to avoid treating traditional discussions of the Buddha's qualities as mythical, symbolic, or a pious fiction. The same is true for any accounts or texts that are determined by prevailing standards of rationality to include elements of magic or depend on miracles. From the perspective of an outsider to Western culture like myself, this ready rejection of the supernatural is somewhat amusing, for contemporary ways of thinking rely just as heavily on miracles and magic as any other tradition of knowledge. The only difference is that they are not acknowledged as such.

Factors Leading to Distortion

From a traditional Dharma perspective, several factors in the academic style of inquiry are almost certain to lead to distortion or misunderstanding of the Dharma, no matter how personally sympathetic that individual may be to Buddhism. First, in studying the teachings of the Buddha and the great masters, it is vital to take into account the context in which their words are spoken or written. To do this requires a comprehensive and coherent view of the Dharma, so that teachings at different levels can be understood as complementary and brought into harmony. Unfortunately the strong tendency among Western scholars is to specialize in a single area, and the scholar who risks doing otherwise is likely to be sharply criticized. Under these conditions, the kind of coherent view necessary for deeper understanding is not likely to develop.

Another limiting factor is that contemporary academic discourse thrives on controversy. The more skillfully one can contest an established view, find apparent contradictions among different teachings, or put forward a novel interpretation that departs from what has traditionally been considered true, the better it is for one's academic career. Such a perspective makes it very difficult to develop the respectful attitude toward the teachings that has traditionally been regarded as essential for understanding their inner significance. It also encourages scholars to take and defend a position, rather than maintaining a primary commitment to truth. Finally, it leads academics to value 'original' interpretations and theories (in other words, those that depart most strongly from the traditional understanding) much more highly than views that confirm the traditional understanding.

Nor is modern academic life structured to allow for the lengthy and intensive inquiry pursued by

traditional scholars in order to develop a truly integrated view of the teachings. Scholars are beset
with various kinds of administrative concerns and
outside pressures that distract them from their
work. More fundamentally, they are encouraged to
develop firm opinions on difficult topics at a very
early stage in their careers. It is not unusual in university circles to find faculty with only a dozen years
(or even less) of exposure to Buddhist thought publishing works that present their own views. In Tibet,
by way of contrast, it would have been unthinkable
to express views on subtle issues of doctrine or practice without many years of study with acknowledged masters of the lineages.

The Foundation for Knowledge

Traditionally speaking, to be able to operate with
any degree of confidence within the complex systems of Buddhist practice and philosophy requires
extensive training. First, it is necessary to understand in depth the kinds of logic that apply to different kinds of texts and issues. Then there is a
grounding in the terminology and the approach
developed within each subject area, knowledge that
comes only through reading widely and having
the opportunity to study with masters well-versed
in each field. Next comes familiarity with the different levels of meaning—inner, outer, and secret—
employed by the great masters in presenting the
more difficult subjects. For instance, it is well

known that in some texts passages have been deliberately rearranged and their meanings concealed, in order to safeguard the text from misuse by those not qualified to work with it. The key required to decode the text is passed on in the oral lineage, so that instruction by a lama is essential.

Assuming this training has been undertaken and a certain level of proficiency reached, the meaning of the texts will still remain opaque unless one is deeply engaged in meditation. In contrast to academic forms of discourse, Buddhist texts need to be interpreted in light of specific meditative practices, for in many cases the meaning of a text will be clear only to those who have cultivated a certain way of operating mind. Put simply, the perception of the Bodhisattva is not the same as the perception of the ordinary individual, and the perception of the Buddha differs from both. This does not mean that one cannot study Dharma without having first stepped onto the Bodhisattva path, but it does suggest that the full meaning of what is studied may not reveal itself to academic styles of analysis, even when such analysis is based on careful linguistic treatment grounded in several canonical languages.

As an example of why the proper understanding of a Buddhist text depends on a truly comprehensive perspective, consider a work in the śāstra tradition. Often a root text or śāstra will consist of a summary or outline, written to distill the essential meaning. A fuller statement of the meaning would be given in additional texts, which might take into account the tradition from which the text originated, compare different interpretive lineages, discuss various philosophical approaches, or reconcile a particular meaning or interpretation with teachings or approaches found in certain classes of Sūtras or śāstras. A text may be analyzed in terms of the three trainings, the four schools, relative or ultimate truth, definitive or provisional meanings, and so on. A particular text might be interpreted in accord with the system of the Abhisamayālaṁkāra or the Mahāyānasūtrālaṁkāra, or explicated with regard to specific distinctions between the Second and Third Dharmacakras.

Writers who entered into this stream of interpretation would follow the lineage that passed through Nāgārjuna and Āryadeva or the lineage in which Asaṅga transmitted the teachings of Maitreya. Some commentators might emphasize the works of Vasubandhu, Candrakīrti, or Candragomin, while others would look to other authorities for guidance. Approaches vary depending on whether the text being studied belonged to the Sūtra, śāstra, or pramāṇa traditions. Finally, the great masters of each school of Tibetan Buddhism developed their own interpretations of the śāstra teachings in major bodies of work, carefully distinguishing their views from those of other commentators.

Interwoven with all these subtleties is the more fundamental issue of how the language of a text is to be understood. For a scholar trained in Western ways of thinking, it might seem adequate to attempt to unravel the literal meaning of a text, but in the Dharma tradition, a text may have many levels of meaning simultaneously (like a work regarded as a literary masterpiece in the West). Here the importance of meditative realization comes to the fore. Even for a text not directly concerned with knowledge that arises from meditative practice, meanings implicit in the language of the text may be clear only when the text is approached in the light of meditative experience.

The tradition itself warns of these subtleties. An example is the famous principle of interpretation that one must always rely on the meaning of the text rather than the meaning of the words, rely on perception based on yogic realization rather than on perception based on ordinary ways of seeing, and rely on communication that conveys enlightened insight and intention rather than the message transmitted by language alone.

Westerners have a further hurdle to surmount, based on the enormous language barriers that bar a correct and comprehensive understanding of the Dharma. Finding the proper equivalents for Dharma terms in modern Western languages is going to take some time, and if students are not willing to adopt a holistic approach to the Dharma, it may not happen at all. Until an adequate vocabulary is developed for each of the many types of Dharma teachings, attempts to convey the meaning of individual works or specific attainments are highly unlikely to succeed. Without this solid grounding, interpretations remain simply speculations, no matter how sophisticated the vocabulary in which they are couched.

Nor can this difficulty be surmounted by reading texts in ther original language, even when a scholar has mastered one or more of the other canonical languages. Although this is certainly helpful, certain issues of translation cannot be so easily set aside. The transmission of meaning is not just a question of translating from one language to another (a matter of finding the right vocabulary or terminology), but of translating Dharma mind into ordinary mind and vice-versa. Translation at this level depends on direct realization—on actually knowing what the text is talking about. Until such realization has been attained, the meaning of a text will be covered over by the layers of rhetoric that samsaric mind imposes. Even though a scholar may be quite familiar with a term in the original canonical languages, he or she will understand it on the basis of samsaric patterns, and such understanding invariably leads to misunderstanding. Misunderstandings can themselves be fruitful, but only if they are understood as approximations, 'stand-ins' for the true meaning that emerges from deeper realization.

To the extent they concede such difficulties, academics may still claim that they can bring to the interpretation of a text a special authority based on their mastery of several canonical languages. There is certainly value in developing this kind of expertise, but I have been surprised by the narrow perspective that Western scholars often take on this point.

For example, some Western scholars hold that the masters of the Tibetan tradition had an imperfect understanding of the Sanskrit originals with which they worked, and that modern academics, whose knowledge of Sanskrit is presumed to be more complete, are therefore justified in dismissing the interpretations made by scholars of the Tibetan schools. Personally, I doubt that this claim can be justified. Western academics who study Sanskrit are trained almost exclusively in the tradition of Pāṇini, while in Tibet scholars had access to seven additional grammatical works lost in their original: the Indra Vyākaraṇa, the Viśala Vyākaraṇa, the Śakautayana Vyākaraṇa, the Samantabhadra Vyākaraṇa, the Patañjali Vyākaraṇa, the Manujanendra Vyākaraṇa, and the Sarasvatī Vyākaraṇa. Moreover, the Buddhist use of language and terms differs quite sharply from their use in Hindu texts, a distinction that Western methods of analysis may not always make clear. Further, the great paṇḍitas of the eighth and ninth centuries and later times, and the Tibetan masters who worked with them to translate the Dharma into Tibetan, were expert in both Sanskrit and Tibetan. They also brought to their work a depth of knowledge regarding the meaning of the texts they were translating that would be difficult to match today.

Proceeding with Caution

I have always encouraged my students to join the study of Tibetan or Sanskrit to the study of history and philosophy, and to unite these studies continuously with meditative inquiry. The Dharma encompasses countless forms of practice and numerous schools of thought, each of which must be understood from the perspective of all the Yānas or vehicles. Without a holistic approach that allows all these elements to come into play, attempts to make sense of a particular teaching or tradition will be like the fable of the blind men who tried to determine the real nature of an elephant.

It is especially sad when scholars who have not developed this kind of comprehensive understanding make pronouncements about the meaning and authenticity of the Dharma. Even if they acknowledge their limited and fragmentary understanding of the tradition, this does not prevent them from propounding their views or publishing their translations. Most disturbing is when scholars publish works that reject the accumulated insights of the great masters of the tradition, as if to say that they understand the Dharma better than the paṇḍitas and lamas who devoted their entire lives to such issues. In my own experience, Westerners are not more intelligent, more spiritually advanced, or more knowledgeable with regard to Dharma than Tibetans, so it is difficult to justify such claims, even when they are left unspoken.

Of course, these dangers are also present for those who do not formally enter the academic world, for the models that support such position-taking are deeply ingrained in the Western mind. Perhaps the best advice for Dharma students is to follow the example of the great Dharma masters, who studied and practiced so extensively and with such great devotion to the lineage. Such scholars seldom made claims regarding their own knowledge; when they offered interpretations of the Dharma, they did so on the basis of thorough investigation and direct realization. Traditionally, it is said that the more one understands the vastness of the Dharma, the more readily a genuine humility takes root in the heart. Where such humility operates, the Dharma will be protected and its value preserved for the future.

A Fundamental Obstacle

The principal handicap for Western scholars who attempt to comprehend the Dharma is the assumption, central to scholarly Western thinking, that knowledge comes through facing outward toward the object of inquiry, rather than through turning inward to explore the workings of the mind that knows. Adopting this view means relying on intellectual rather than experiential knowledge, for it is precisely the intellectual and conceptual mind that treats the object of knowledge as being located somewhere else, separate from the knower. When it comes to Dharma study, however, an exclusive reliance on the tools of the intellectual mind can only inhibit real insight and understanding.

Conceptual understanding can be a valuable means for fostering insight, yet certain types of knowledge central to Buddhist teachings simply cannot be 'pieced together' or 'puzzled out' using ordinary logic and perceptions. Inquiry that depends too strongly on a proliferating web of concepts may actually interfere with understanding the inner meaning of a text or a teaching. Understanding comes only when the mind learns to relax into the qualities of an enlightened way of being, expanding into its own fullness and sinking into its own depth. It is the turning inward to direct experience, not conceptual, object-centered investigation, that makes this different way of knowing available.

The Buddha called on human beings to replace their present way of life with one grounded in realization, making every effort to replace samsaric understanding with enlightened significance. He did not aim solely at explaining how things are, but went on to show how we can change the way *we* are. If we approach the Dharma without being willing to put our own way of being at stake, we close our hearts to this intention. When that is so—when we refuse to let the Dharma serve its purpose—how can its meaning be accurately comprehended?

For instance, to understand the nature of the Buddha means to understand the special virtues and qualities of enlightened being. But this is possible only when one accepts the Buddha as an Enlightened Master. Put differently, the way to understand who the Buddha *is* is to develop faith in the Tathāgata as the Guide for the World, taking inspiration from the Buddha's presence, his story, and his teachings so that appreciation for the qualities of enlightenment can enter the heart and mind. Ultimately, understanding the Dharma depends on opening to its blessings. To take the position of an outsider, judging the Dharma in terms of one's own values, is to seal off its meaning. It is not just a question of missing some subtle nuance or added layer—taking this approach obscures the teachings at the most fundamental level.

In this context, even a sincere commitment to knowledge is not enough, because knowledge in a Dharma sense is very different from the knowledge that the academic pursues. Since knowledge as it unfolds on the path calls into question the identity of the one who knows, there is no way for the individual to own or acquire it. In the end, each insight, each creative advance, must be acknowledged as the very voice of the Buddha: the Dharma speaking within the mind. To claim otherwise, to believe that one can observe Buddhism from a distance, bringing one's own 'impartial' intelligence to bear, is to ensure that the meaning of the teachings will not be successfully transmitted.

In Dharma study, we cannot stand in two places at once: our heart cannot be in one place and our mind in another. Trying to do so introduces waves of confusion: confused models, confused objectives, confused interpretations, and confusion in others. As the tide of confusion rises, the only safe place to retreat is into skepticism. At that point, conceptual insight becomes a way to withdraw from the teachings still further. The chance to benefit personally or to help others through careful inquiry into the Dharma disappears, and with it the chance to understand what the Dharma is all about.

From an academic perspective, the claim that the teachings of the Buddha reveal what it means to be a human being is just one among many aspects of Buddhist doctrine to be studied. But this 'objective' way of treating the Dharma is self-contradictory. The Dharma is a path, and only by taking it can this path be understood.

To put this point most strongly, it is not possible to understand Buddhism unless one is a Buddhist who has integrated the teachings and merged them into deeply held convictions. The meaning of the Dharma, as passed on by the living lineage, cannot be handed over to someone who maintains the stance of the objective observer, firmly convinced that there is no higher knowledge than the knowledge that is 'mine'. Yet the discipline imposed on Western academics as part of their training insists on just this approach.

That is why Dharma students who attempt to make their home in the academic world face such great difficulty, and why, despite their good intentions, their published studies and translations must be approached with caution. Here, as in all other aspects of the path, the best support is deep respect for the tradition, nourished by a comprehensive training that combines academic study with meditative practice and with the firm resolve to embody the teachings in all that one does.

The Therapeutic Approach
and Beyond

The present time is a fortunate one, for the Dharma is becoming more widely available. Yet it is also a time of great mental instability. The patterns of neurosis we see operating in others, or perhaps in ourselves, hint that there are forces driving us that we cannot clearly comprehend or identify. The emotional disorders that afflict so many in our society suggest that the path we have collectively chosen to follow is not well-suited to promoting health and well-being.

Caught up in the busy-ness of our times, many people have the sense of being trapped on a treadmill, pressured in both their private and working lives, and troubled by a feeling that it will never be possible to catch up with time. They may respond with sensations of panic or by blocking off all sensations; they may experience tremendous stress, confusion, and tension, or fall back into cynicism and a restless search for new forms of entertainment. Anxiety, depression, and low self-esteem are the epidemics of our age, as pervasive and in some ways as deadly as the epidemics that ravaged whole populations in other times and places.

Aware that the knowledge that frames our convictions and beliefs is not nearly as securely grounded as we like to imagine, many individuals in the modern world are sensitized to the danger of being manipulated, psychologically abused, or deceived by others. But from a Dharma perspective, we are all already the victims of a pervasive manipulation—a kind of brainwashing set into operation before our consciousness took form. If we doubt that this is so, we can simply ask: Do we know why we hold the values we do? Do we know why society rejects as false the truths that operated in the past, and adopts others in their place? Do we truly imagine that we as individuals have much say in these matters?

Long ago we were seduced into making fundamental choices that have shaped our way of life. Now, as we struggle to make the best of our situation, we are the victims of those choices. Like a reservoir, we collect the influences that rain down on us and distribute them to others. The passivity of our role in this current tends to erode vision and creativity, rendering us uncertain and disconnected. As a result, all of us have times when we wonder whether our striving and effort serve any higher purpose. But if we are unable to conceive of a viable alternative, we have little choice but to push ahead toward a goal we cannot bring into clear focus.

When we have no clear system of moral values to guide us and no shared sense of a spiritual path to give order to our lives, it is nearly impossible to maintain balance amidst the turmoils of our modern ways of life. If we do not retreat into passivity, we may find ourselves lurching from one view to another and from one circumstance to another in search of fulfillment. But with no real guidance, our search for happiness rarely reaches a point of rest and contentment. When we recognize these patterns at work within and around us, it can seem that a shadow has fallen across human destiny, obscuring the light of knowledge and imprinting its darkness on our hearts and minds.

The Therapeutic Response

Western therapeutic models attempt to respond to these patterns and concerns in a variety of ways. By seeking to understand and help others understand the patterns that shape and control our minds, therapists have been able to assist many people who would otherwise have fallen deeper into suffering.

Still, the kinds of understanding that Western psychology offers have their own difficulties and limitations. For instance, labeling a certain condition or state of mind as a mental disorder automatically restricts the power of the mind to work out its own liberation. Once the label has been applied, a problem has been defined and set in place. Now the creative energy of the mind must be channeled toward solving this problem, instead of toward looking at experience just as it is. This kind of problem solving is time-consuming and expensive, and clinicians are increasingly pressured to rely on drugs as a simple and immediate solution. But this does little more than conceal the problem.

Psychotherapy operates by looking for explanations of mental disorders and tracing out how a particular problem developed. This approach may indeed suggest possible cures, but it has a major and little noticed side effect. When we look for the cause that led to a particular difficulty, we guarantee that the more fundamental structures that establish the cause/effect relationship will never be called into question. At this level, there is no impetus to explore the structures and dynamics of mind and consciousness (except perhaps at the level of brain chemistry and physiology). Unnoticed or dismissed, these structures and dynamics remain essentially invisible.

In the past few decades, some therapists, together with individuals exploring on their own, have become aware of such limitations. In their search for alternatives, a substantial number of therapists have discovered that the teachings of the Buddha offer the potential for deeper insight into the workings of mind. In particular, they have realized that Buddhist meditation offers a way to investigate directly how the mind operates, how consciousness can be transformed, and how people can be encouraged to find meaning in their lives. Today many mental health professionals study and practice Buddhist teachings on formal meditation, mindfulness and compassion, as well as methods for integrating body and mind. Some Buddhist teachers also emphasize this therapeutical approach, convinced that this is the way that the Dharma can be of the most immediate benefit to Western students.

This approach may indeed prove deeply valuable. Yet unless it is grounded in a more radical inquiry, one that systematically investigates the whole of the mental realm and its workings, the continuing focus on the patterns of ordinary mind may distort the teachings. For the Dharma does not aim at changing the patterns of ordinary mind: its goal is to transform these patterns into the truth of enlightened being.

A Buddhist Approach

Buddhism's vast wealth of teachings on the nature of mind is almost impossible to describe. Starting from the analysis of mind and mental events found in the Abhidharma teachings and the profound insights into the nature of existence conveyed in the Prajñāpāramitā, the schools known as Cittamātra, Vijñānavāda, and Mādhyamika undertook a detailed analysis of how the mind operates, beginning with the sense fields and faculties and the interplay of thoughts, feelings, and emotions, then penetrating to the root of consciousness and beyond. In the Mantrayāna, this analysis was expanded to include the subtle energies that flow through the body and the structures that support and channel them.

If the modern world is to benefit fully from the availability of the Dharma, a careful study of all these elements of the tradition seems vital. Such inquiry will of course be grounded in meditative inquiry, but it is equally important to clarify the theoretical constructs through which we make sense of the mental realm.

At the outset of their analysis, the texts of the Dharma traditions identify many different kinds of mind, including vijñāna, citta, caitta, manas, and ālayavijñāna. They name fifty-one or more mental events, eight kinds of consciousness, and nine ways the mind manifests. These are all fundamental topics to explore, valuable pointers that allow us to refine our understanding at levels that Western psychology does not accommodate.

Since ordinary mind is strongly attuned to the power of naming, the Dharma exercises this naming capacity to the fullest, allowing it to guide us into the nature of mind and offering it new insights, new methods, and new directions to explore. As inquiry deepens, this initial reliance on naming, classifying and identifying experience and tracing out its characteristics, gives way to a kind of knowing less bound to specific forms. Now it may prove difficult to find words for describing the means by which the mind operates, for discovering its characteristics, or for clarifying the relationship between mind and the reality it discloses. Still, when we persist, we can see more clearly how the mind shapes reality, generating one manifestation after another, from surface exhibitions to the very deepest levels of experience. This is how the tapestry of samsara is fabricated and how the chain of karma is forged. It is the the present truth of our lives, and it holds a great fascination.

Yet this is not the whole truth of mind. The Vinaya, Abhidharma, and Prajñāpāramitā all operate on the mind in different ways, and all lead to different insight into its nature. As we explore their teachings, we discover within the mind new realms of expansion, wonderment, and joy. We could describe such exploration as philosophical inquiry integrated with meditative practice, but that is perhaps too limiting. The Buddhist teachings on mind offer a way of developing all our human capacities. That is why the Bodhisattvas focus their efforts on mind, viewing mind as both teacher and student. In this society, where we have advanced so far in studying the material world, the time seems right to follow this same model, this fresh and infinitely promising form of inquiry.

Inquiry into Mind

Buddhism teaches that mind can be our worst enemy or our best friend. It can fool us completely, trapping us in constructs that lead to wasted time, confusion, or misery, while mocking our efforts to achieve our own good; or it can give direct access to all that makes life meaningful. It can strike like a rattlesnake, infecting us with its poison, or it can be our great protector. It has the power to shape our lives, now and in the future. The Dharma masters who learned the nature of mind derived great benefit from this knowledge, and they passed on their attainment to us, so that we too could profit.

Mind as an active presence cannot be detected or captured, although we see its footprints everywhere. In fact, our lives are nothing other than the track laid down by those prints. Yet mind itself is a mystery.

It would be wrong to think that this is the final word. The study of mind is possible; the knowledge of mind is available. When mind rules our lives, what can be more important than such a knowing: not just mapping the operations of mind, but knowing how it is set up and how to regard its claims? To know what the mind means is to know how the mind means, and what this means for us.

To gain an understanding of mind, we need a form of inquiry suited to the nature of its subject matter. If we turn the mind into an object of investigation, as we inspect a tree or a rock, we will see at best the outermost level of its operations—a little like traveling round and round the circumference of a circle. A more suitable method is to examine how the mind interprets mind to itself. We may start like scientists, exploring how mind operates, but we also want to go further: We want to explore the how of that how.

This way of inquiry depends on entering the center of the mind to discover the nature of the one who is investigating. If the mind is not so shy that it withdraws from view, if the ego is not too tender and raw to let itself be touched, this path can unfold almost without effort. Each question becomes its own answer, and each answer opens into new kinds of questions, new realms of knowledge. The understanding that arises in this way goes beyond the subject/object polarity that defines ordinary knowledge. It moves toward the all-encompassing wisdom known in Buddhism as prajñā.

When we look at ordinary mind, what stands out is its complete unreliability. One day we feel one way, the next another; this month we are completely convinced, but next month we have grave doubts. We reach the heights of joy, then fall to the depths of misery; we imagine wonderful accomplishments, then plunge into self-doubt; we awaken to the beauty of life, then go to sleep again. In the face of such changeability, there can be no real security, no guarantees as to where our mind will go next—nothing that is trustworthy.

Although the operations of ordinary mind provide no way out of these patterns, prajñā knows how to make the very instability of mind the path of inquiry. With prajñā, we can make use of every mental event: each thought or emotion, each act of labeling or defining, every field and each variation. As we learn to do this, our ordinary inner environment becomes more stimulating than the best play or exhibition. Each new manifestation is an opportunity to learn more.

More fundamental than the manifestations mind projects is mind itself, which guides us on our path of inquiry as the eyes guide the body. This is mind the seer, the listener, the feeler; mind the decision-maker and adviser. When prajñā is operating, we are attuned to this level. We understand more fully how the endless variations that constitute the content of mind take form, and we find that we are free to experiment with different alternatives, take new roles, and create new models. Masters over mind, we can shape our thoughts and our reactions in more fruitful ways.

The Nature of Mind

The common sense view is that experience as the mind presents it accurately reflects reality. In turn, mind is a part of this reality, poorly understood but largely taken for granted. It is just this initial rather mindless understanding of mind that Buddhism calls into question.

The Cittamātra school of Buddhism, based on analysis of mind and perception, considers all perceptions to be reflections of mind. First the mind receives sensory input, then it imposes meaning on what has been experienced, creating a story that makes sense of the whole. But what story can we tell about mind itself? Standard forms of inquiry cannot say, for the nature of mind is such that we cannot determine its location and assign it a role, as we would with an external object. The alternative that the Cittamātra school suggests is that we learn to see mind reflected in what we have projected, and in the meanings assigned to those projections.

Before this is possible, we must teach the mind to settle down. Most of the time, the mind is caught in a kind of chaotic whirl. One thought gives rise to the next, and emotions surge through our awareness with so much intensity that we cannot gain the clarity to take note of them. With the mind this disordered, we cannot see its workings. But if we learn to relax the mind so that it comes into balance, the basic anxieties and fears that ordinarily condition its responses dissipate. Now the mind can release its tight grip on experience, and we can deal in a positive way with our inner environment. We are ready to ask fundamental questions about the mind's nature and its relation to reality.

For mind to look at mind, projecting mind into mind, a special skill is required, a little like the skills a photographer must develop in order to focus and frame an image. The key is the quality of clarity that emerges when inner calm is available. Such clarity allows each perception to be more fully inclusive, engaging mind as well as what the mind projects.

The knowledge that arises through this inclusive way of perceiving holds the fullness of awareness, making awareness itself available to inquiry—not as the object of inquiry, but as the 'aura' that emanates from mental operations. In the light of this 'aura', it becomes possible to see how the kleśas manifest, how the chain of karma comes into operation, how we identify and accumulate knowledge, and how reality is distributed through conscious and unconscious activity. We see in a new way who we are, and discover, almost effortlessly, how to function in a more coherent and satisfying manner. All this can happen independently of extensive study of the texts, for we are touching our own knowledge and awareness directly, in the closest possible way.

When we are first setting out, all this can seem a bit complicated. For instance, a Buddhist meditation teacher may say to us, "Watch the mind!" But when mind watches mind, do we also have to watch the mind that watches? Is it even possible to watch in both directions at once? We give ourselves an order: Watch the mind! Who is the one who finds that order meaningful and tries to carry it out? Is that someone exempt from being watched? At a deeper level, what is the order that supports the order? Does this 'order of the order' even exist? If so, in what sense is it true? Does it display an 'orderness'? We may have to act as if this were so, to accept it as so, but is this the fact of the matter? On the other hand, if we have no choice in how mind functions, is it worthwhile asking the question?

Such questions can be deeply engaging, leading inquiry in fruitful directions. Gradually we realize that mind is present everywhere, playing every role in each new drama of our lives. There is trouble-making mind; peaceful mind,\; intelligent, advanced mind. There is mind that has transcendent experience of another realm. Then there is the mind that reviews all this, observing, comparing, and commenting. Is this interpreter mind a separate entity? Is it better understood as a byproduct of each successive mental event? Again, mind seems to present the one who acts and the one who directs the action. Which one is responsible? Which one imposes a rule? Can that one be overruled? If so, how? And who is the one that overrules?

The point of asking such questions is not necessarily to arrive at answers. The very experience of closely engaging the mind is deeply refreshing, and that sense of freshness is what counts. It allows us to see our reality and our experience differently and spontaneously releases many of the tensions and concerns with which we usually operate.

Beyond Relative Mind

On the relative level of ordinary appearance, whatever manifests could be said to depend on being filtered through the mind. Sense impressions, the felt sense of the body, intuition, and the happenings of our lives are all communicated to us in this way. The interpreter and the interpretation are both inseparable from mind; 'subject' and 'object' equally depend on it. Even the experience that lets us develop the concept 'mind' is pronounced through mind.

Is there also a level apart from the relative, a level at which mind might not function at all? Reflecting on the qualities of the Buddha suggests that the answer is yes. Though the texts sometimes use the term 'enlightened mind', that may only be a manner of speaking, for the omniscience of the Buddha, which has to do with an all-pervasive knowledge, does not seem linked to mind at all.

The Mahāyāna speaks of enlightened mind as bodhicitta, and offers the practice of the six perfections as the means for arriving at the wisdom and compassion that are its distinguishing characteristics. While we might think of bodhicitta as a 'new' mind, a more accurate description would be to say that bodhicitta has always been the nature of mind itself, expressing the highest qualities of absolute perfection. Inseparable from prajñā, neither established nor sponsored, bodhicitta overarches existence as the unity of the Dharmadhātu. At this most fundamental level, mind dissolves into light.

In enlightened awareness, appearance (which for the Cittamātra is inseparable from mind) is transformed into pervasive openness. In the Middle Way understanding of the Mādhyamika school, this is expressed by saying that the mind itself is empty (śūnya). However, 'emptiness' (śūnyatā) in turn must be carefully analyzed. Śūnyatā is not empty in the sense of being a negation or an absence. It does not involve 'departing from' what exists or 'being something else'. Śūnyatā negates the 'from/to' orientation on which ordinary negation—which upholds the patterns of ordinary mind—is based.

Suppose you find yourself the guest in a house. Naturally you assume that the house exists—that it has a history, which is accessible to inquiry. From the perspective of śūnyatā, however, the history that 'accounts' for the house may not establish its existence at all. Perhaps the house (together with its history) has never been built. In answer to this charge, your host steps forward to insist that the house is real. Very well, but who will be the witness for the existence of the host? Again, you are there as guest, enjoying your stay. But what will serve to establish your existence?

Once the orienting factors of 'from' and 'to' on which we ordinarily rely are called into question, there is no use in attempting to establish anything on the basis of something else. To establish—to make comparisons between existence and non-existence—we must first have a reference point. But how can there be such a point without 'from' and 'to'? If we think of the reference point as 'zero', we could ask in this way: How can there be a zero that establishes zero?

Points of reference clearly serve a purpose. Once we have a point 'here', we can distinguish this point from what is 'not here'. The 'not' in this 'not here' marks out a certain kind of emptiness or absence, and this mode of establishing makes possible the juxtapositions out of which the relative realm that mind knows is built up. But this identified emptiness, born of the 'here', is not śūnyatā. Nor is śūnyatā the emptiness that is not this emptiness, for in that case this 'ultimate' śūnyatā would again depend on something that was prior to śūnyatā. We can no more arrive at śūnyatā in this way than we could do away with the opposite side of a coin by slicing the coin into ever thinner slices. The emptiness of śūnyatā does not empty that which was previously full. If we must rely on words, we might say that śūnyatā is the whole that encompasses both 'empty' and 'full'. Alternatively, we might say that śūnyatā is the absolute, but then we must add that this absolute is nothing other than the relative.

The difficulty in making sense of śūnyatā is that we inevitably find ourselves drawing on distinctions taken from the realm of existents (including the category 'non-existent'). This vocabulary, so closely tied to our relative way of 'minding', is inadequate to śūnyatā. By the same token, if our relative way of 'minding' were to cease, so that śūnyatā came to the fore, our way of being—our way 'to be'—would become something other than what we are presently able to express.

Applying this analysis to mind, we might say that mind is the authority that specifies the nature of existence and non-existence: not because the mind reserves to itself the power to define, but because mind cognizes in a characteristic way, perceiving and thus determining what can appear. In cognizing, mind pronounces, and as that pronouncement takes effect, it becomes the sign of what constitutes—for us—a true fact. Since mind also immediately reads what has been pronounced, a characteristic exchange is established: mind transmitting mind to mind.

Based on this analysis, is it more accurate to say that mind is two or mind is one, or perhaps that mind echoes mind? The question has no answer. Mind alone could be the witness to any such distinction, but there is no third mind to play that role. Once the pronouncement has been made, our minds are made up. What happens after that must remain indeterminate, for the road that leads past that point is too narrow to allow access to the vehicle of the intellect. We are free to speculate, but there seems no way to arrive at the intrinsic introspection that would allow us to know this more subtle body of mind.

To escape this dead end, we must develop a more sophisticated knowledge. The model that tells us that reality arises as mind transmits mind is two-dimensional. Could we move into a different dimension? For instance, what if we dropped the focus on the *outcome* of our 'minding', and looked instead at the *qualities* of 'minding'? While language may hint at alternatives, no answer to the question is possible. To arrive at this 'essential' knowledge, philosophical mind, like common-sense mind and perception mind, needs the assistance of a more complete way of understanding. In the end we must cultivate the special clarity of meditation guided by insight.

Emptiness Mind

Consider the notion that the universe has a point of origin in space and time. If we say that before the origin, nothing existed, we might consider that 'nothing' to be śūnya. In the same way, if the universe comes to an end, what happens after that end might be śūnya as well. But in that case—if the universe originates in śūnya and ends in śūnya—how can the universe as it exists 'in between' be anything 'more' than śūnya? It is like the contents of the dream we will have tonight: at this moment, the contents of the dream do not exist, and when we wake up tomorrow they will also not exist. Then will they exist while the dream is occurring?

On the other hand, the very idea of 'between' implies a substantial basis. If we want to step away entirely from such a basis, can we say anything at all? If not, how we can ever determine what śūnyatā is? Perhaps we cannot: Perhaps there are no adjectives, no basis for comparison—not even the fall-back position 'indeterminate'.

For someone who approaches the Dharma in terms of Western-oriented psychology, all this may seem like needless complications. Why not be satisfied with developing greater awareness of mind in operation, with fostering more patience with the mind, so that mind can grow more flexible? Why not aim to develop happy mind, open mind, tranquil mind, sharp mind, clear mind, aware mind? Why not establish greater peace of mind, and leave it at that? These are topics we can take hold of, because they make sense to us.

Even at this practical level, it can be worthwhile to go deeper in our questioning. Watching the mind in meditation can have a therapeutic effect, but sooner or later we are likely to fall into a cloudy or dull kind of awareness that can trap us for extended periods. At that point, a more fundamental questioning that exercises the thinking capacity of mind can be a way of waking up—a way of reminding ourselves that this matter of the mind is serious business. It is actually not that hard to fool ourselves in our meditation practice, but if we are ready to question experience more deeply, looking to see how our reality is constructed, we will stay more alert to such self-deception. When we can see how our usual understanding shapes the way we make up our mind, we are close to knowing the body of mind. As the quality of mind begins to shine through our meditation, meditation becomes a reliable resource for illumination and inspiration, a fruitful path for understanding the meaning of life.

From this perspective, the significance of śūnyatā as 'less' (or 'more') than indeterminate is that mind may be similarly indeterminate. If we pursue our inquiry into this mind, we arrive at a 'psychology' of emptiness, one that does not depend on the patterns of my mind or your mind, but on the universal attributes of mind. By developing this 'emptiness' mind, we come closer to the universal qualities of the Enlightened Ones, which stand at the center of the Dharma.

This shift has fundamental importance. As long as we insist on a basis from which mind can investigate mind, we are unlikely to arrive at a final understanding of how the mind operates. But when there is no such basis, every instant and every pattern becomes available to knowledge. We can see how emotionality arises; we can eliminate our dependence on patterns that were already in operation before we were born. We can refuse to be hypnotized by the messages that float through our heads and assault our senses. We can transcend the tendency for confusion to reflect itself forward into the future, like an echo that never dies away.

When the mind gains access to such 'emptiness knowledge', it becomes self-enlightening. We no longer find ourselves in the impossible position of trying to use samsaric mind to arrive at the truth of the Dharma. We could say that the problems that ordinary mind knows so well disappear, but it is more accurate to say that problems simply cannot arise, because they cannot 'take place'. The shift is subtle: a slight alteration in the way we understand appearance and mind. Yet this modest change gives us a new way to be. As the limits on our awareness fall away, we become a different person. We might think of śūnyatā as the aspirin that relieves a headache we were born with: the headache of sam-sara, which has defined our being for longer than any of us knows.

There is also a danger here. Śūnyatā, like any-thing else, can become something we think about rather than embody. The texts of the tradition, aware of this trap, are constantly inviting us to clar-ify our understanding of what śūnyatā is and is not. Depending on the method of analysis, they identify eighteen kinds of śūnyatā, or twelve, or four, or three. Following their lead, we realize the need to refine our understanding at every turn, relying on the guidance made available by the Buddha and the great masters of the past.

Creativity of Mind

The West has its own tradition of actively engaging the mind. It draws on mind's creative power through art and science, philosophy and innovation. While this tradition tends to focus on the products of mind, it can also be applied to investigate mind directly. In the beginning we may proceed intellectually, but eventually we discover that the mind can make room for meditative realization, and that meditation in turn can create room for the mind. At that point the gateway to 'emptiness mind' is not so distant.

When we explore the mind through meditation, we are like an artist who relies on intuition to shape raw materials into a work of art. But we can do more. When we learn to bring meditation into balance with insight, we can shape the creative vision of meditation to achieve far more powerful and meaningful results. As artists of the mind, we can use the insights made available by the Dharma science of mind to create symbols that help unlock deeper levels of meaning. The beauty of realization and the spontaneous power of śūnyatā can manifest in the shapes and forms that the mind produces, giving appearance itself a powerful aesthetic dimension. We can embody the beauty of appearance and exercise the wisdom of the highest knowledge.

Appreciation for the wonders of the mind translates into a reverence for the sentient beings who manifest mind, and for the world of appearance that gives it form. Instead of distorting or distracting one another with their competing claims, subject and object can sustain a mutual dance of realization: object acknowledging its own appearance as the play of mind, and subject respecting what appears as the symbol of a reality more fundamental than its own constructs. The beauty of this mutual reflection expresses the openness of śūnyatā. It furthers a playful creativity, guided and inspired by the highest knowledge, known in the Buddhist traditions as līla.

The more we exercise such knowledge, the more readily we can create a world of ever greater beauty and joy. Worries and fear and the sense that something is missing fade away, and we act instead out of compassion—and also for the sheer pleasure of creating something of value. Because our efforts naturally bring benefits to others, our life here on earth becomes richly meaningful. Practicing the six perfections, we steadily transform samsara into realization. Working for posterity, we reap the benefits in joy and a lightness of being. Our perspectives, our embodiment, and our behavior all change completely. Living fully, producing fully, engaging fully, we move beyond the concerns of psychology, beyond the realm of ordinary mind. We savor the pleasure of each moment as we might luxuriously sample the dishes in a wonderful restaurant. Life becomes an ongoing celebration.

The Dharma Way of Work

Many Tibetan teachers now regularly make visits to the West and to other countries where interest in Tibetan Buddhism is growing. Offering teachings and blessings, they are welcomed by friendly audiences with a lively curiosity about Tibet and Buddhist teachings. Clearly such visits have real value, and it may be that they plant the karmic seeds that will eventually mature into a deeper Dharma connection.

Still, my own feeling is that such brief visits do not go far enough toward supporting students who have or who might develop a serious interest in the Dharma. Wearing a red protection cord is not enough to make someone a Buddhist. If the teachings are to take root in the West, lamas must be willing to work with Westerners and other interested students on a daily basis.

Integrating Dharma teachings into every aspect of life is an ongoing project. It requires substantial effort on the part of the student, but also a continuing involvement on the part of the teacher. Is this really happening today? For instance, how many lamas with Western students make the effort to understand Western history and culture, Western psychology and philosophy, and Western styles of communication? Perhaps some lamas consider that this is not necessary, but based on my experience, I would say that without some kind of shared background, the basis for a deep interaction will be difficult to establish.

Many Tibetan lamas who travel abroad do not seem to treat their foreign students in the same way they treat their Tibetan disciples. Often they project an image of great sweetness and charm. Of course, this can be quite useful. But the Buddha taught that there are four methods for developing disciples in the Dharma: generosity, sweet words, having a common purpose, and helpful activity. For the teacher to assist the student in forming a genuine bond to the Dharma, all four of these should be engaged. Sweet words can be the basis for a mutually gratifying connection between teacher and student, but for the connection to deepen, the student must be given the chance to learn what it means to make a true commitment to the Dharma.

It is dangerous to allow new Dharma students to imagine that a qualified Tibetan teacher can distribute spiritual attainments to students as a school teacher might distribute candy to schoolchildren, for sooner or later that sweetness will dissipate. Perhaps some lamas simply do not think that Westerners have the capacity for making the kind of whole-hearted commitment that will ensure progress on the journey to enlightenment, but I would not be quick to make that judgment.

Such questions have been of continuing concern to me from the time I arrived in the West more than thirty years ago. For most of a decade, I experimented with different ways to present the tradition and teachings in a new land. To my students, I taught basic Dharma concepts and practices; for the general public, I established the Nyingma Institute, where I focused on interacting with professionals, religious leaders, and educators to explore the possibilities for shared understanding.

After almost ten years of such activities, I felt that I had gone far enough in this direction. Since then I have done very little teaching in public. Instead, I have focused on working closely with a small group of students, encouraging them to deepen their involvement with the Dharma as a way of life. I cannot say whether these interactions have brought any of us closer to enlightenment, but I do know that our work together has made a contribution to the preservation of the Dharma. And I am satisfied that to work with this intention is itself an aspect of the Buddhist path.

The Benefits of Dharma Work

The Buddha taught with great precision how to proceed toward enlightenment. The ten stages of the Bodhisattva path and the five paths that lead to perfect realization can guide us toward transcending our own suffering and transforming the suffering of others. In the past, great Bodhisattvas and accomplished masters drew on these teachings to work for the benefit of all beings. While we cannot hope to match their attainments, we too can learn to direct our efforts toward the welfare of others in our own limited way. The practice we have evolved for doing this is one we call Skillful Means—using work as a way to practice the Dharma.

Making Dharma work the path toward knowledge and transformation will not appeal to everyone. Students who joined our community in the early days did not necessarily foresee that this would be their path, and some of them later left because they wanted to pursue other approaches. Even today students sometimes ask me how much longer we will have to keep on working so hard, and when we will be able to shift instead to 'real' Dharma practice. My reply is that what we are doing *is* real Dharma practice. Certainly we do not claim that our work offers a quick and easy path to higher realization. But it does offer the opportunity to learn through direct experience what the tradition is, how to connect to it, and what it means to serve the Dharma.

The projects we have taken on as a community make great demands on all of us. Our resources are limited, our goals vast, and our numbers small. To meet the shifting requirements of our work, we have had to learn dozens of new skills, from teaching, management, publishing, and printing, to construction, maintenance, art, and architecture, to planning, design, finances, and much more. But this is exactly where the opportunity for transformation comes in. As we take on these challenges, we are also challenging our own beliefs about our limitations. We are expanding what we are able to accomplish and learning to set aside personal interests for the sake of the goals we all have in common. These inner challenges, which inevitably trigger stubborn resistance, offer real insight into the workings of samsara and the mental patterns that fuel suffering. They also let us explore in a heartfelt way the methods that the teachings make available to overcome pain and frustration.

For example, when it begins to seem impossible to get the desired result or meet the deadlines we have set for a particular project, we have a chance to test the depth and quality of our commitment. We have learned that if we can touch our own deepest resolve, we can do far more than we thought. The difficulties we encounter enable us to measure and improve our ability, our motives, and our understanding. The simple fact that we do not give up in the face of adversity, or shift our energy into making excuses for failure, helps strengthen our conviction.

As long as we do not give up, we can be confident that through this experience, we are building our skills and our capacities for the next time.

Working for the Dharma gives us the opportunity to cultivate vigor and patience, inner discipline, and a deep appreciation for beauty in its most refined forms. Through the practice of the six perfections, we can learn to be consistent in our action and firm in our resolve. By cultivating compassion and selflessness, we can generate the energy and insight to sustain to the best of our capacity the qualities of enlightened creativity.

As our community has learned what it means to develop inner discipline and exercise abilities beyond what anyone thought possible, our lives have become very rich. We have seen that vīrya, the practice of intense and focused effort, transforms directly into knowledge. We have discovered through our own experience that once human beings find themselves in circumstances that favor Dharma activity, their potential is limitless. We have learned that we can see through the limitations, fabrications, and deceptions of ordinary mind and its self-centered logic. In our own small way, we have glimpsed how it is that Gautama Śākyamuni, the prince of the Śākyas, became the perfectly enlightened Buddha.

To work for the Dharma means letting go of the idea that our efforts will lead us directly to spiritual attainment. As a discipline founded in awareness and dedication and directed toward the welfare of others, the work has its own intrinsic value. If we let this realization take root, the knowledge that what we do will have benefits for posterity evokes a deep sense of fulfillment. We might call this a religious path, but we could just as well call it a humanitarian path, a compassionate path, a path of knowledge—even a path of wisdom.

Facing up to Obstacles

Today the very concept of selfless action strikes many people as foolish or even self-contradictory. Such skepticism has an impact, making our task that much harder. Whenever we do begin to develop a Dharma perspective, friends and family become the spokespersons for lingering doubts and inner conflicts. They are eager to tell us that we are wasting our time, that our priorities are mistaken, that we have to look out for ourselves, that we are giving too much or have lost our sense of perspective. Since the models for how it is possible to live a Dharma life in the modern world do not yet exist, it is difficult to reply to such well-meaning but destructive advice in ways that others can understand.

Working with positive energy, developing awareness of our shortcomings and the belief systems that support them, and striving to change the patterns that hold us in samsara will eventually result in change at a deep level. However, no one should expect that it will be easy. Without the support of a culture centered on the Dharma, individuals new to the teachings are at the mercy of countless influences that undermine their commitment. The messages we hear in the media or the views we hear from our friends invite us to turn our backs on what we know to have value. Still more dangerous are the trusted voices in our heads, activated long ago and without our consent, that insist that we are fine the way we are, that blame others for our difficulties, or that offer up a steady stream of distracting thoughts and fantasies. In the face of such powerful forces, it is difficult to focus on what has real meaning and value.

There is an ancient story about a king who learned from his ministers that the water in his kingdom had become poisoned, and that anyone who drank it would take leave of his senses. Fortunately, the king had a private well that had not been affected, and thus he himself stayed sane. But after a time, his subjects, who had totally lost their minds, began to complain about the king, saying that he was no longer a fit ruler, and that he followed ways that harmed the people. For a long time, the king persisted, trying to guide his people and care for their needs, but in the end he had no choice: he too had to drink the poisoned water.

Sometimes I feel that those who hold to the path of the Dharma find themselves in a similar situation. To see clearly what is happening, and especially to see how much harm people do to themselves totally unaware, can be deepy distressing.

Persevering in Practice

Despite such obstacles, the deeper we go in Skillful Means practice, the more self-evident its value becomes, and the more we begin to realize that it truly is possible to transform the mind. To give to the Dharma, working to protect and transmit the teachings, putting aside our own ambitions and desires for the sake of others, is perhaps the most effective way of all to gain knowledge of what the tradition really stands for. Whatever the specifics of our work, we are practicing the six perfections. As the symbols we create and the works we produce take on shape and substance, the mandala of realization takes form in our hearts.

The benefits of this way of work are felt throughout our community. Those who have participated in creating the Odiyan mandala have grown to appreciate the significance of the monuments and sacred symbols they have helped bring into being. Those who have helped establish and refine the complementary mandala of the Nyingma organizations are better equipped than anyone else to understand the vision that has guided the creation and growth of our community. The more students set aside personal concerns and give priority to helping preserve and transmit the Dharma, the more they strengthen their ability to deepen their understanding of the Buddhist teachings.

Dharma Work and Business

Often I have thought that the lessons we have learned through our work should be useful in any field of endeavor, even when no Dharma motivation is in operation. In the mid-1980s, several Nyingma community members who shared this conviction formed a company called Skillful Means Enterprises, which was succeeded a few years later by Dharma Enterprises. Their aim was to draw upon the special path of knowledge through work that we had developed and set an example for others by applying it in a demanding, production-oriented business setting. Despite some initial difficulties in making the transition to the competitive business world, these operations were quite successful, a result I attribute to the steady refinement and implementation of the Skillful Means path.

When individuals in a work setting can avoid the snares of emotionality and negativity, they can produce to their full potential, which gives them a tremendous advantage. When they learn to cultivate awareness, concentration, and energy, their work becomes creative and fulfilling: the expression of a new and more enriching space-time dynamic.

In one sense, the values cultivated in the business world are quite different from Dharma values. But at another level, the teachings of the Dharma can be applied in any situation. Awareness, concentration, and energy are central to all human activity, and the special working ethics that we call Skillful

Means should be valuable for anyone who wants to be effective, achieve good results, and find more meaning in work. Perhaps in the future it will be possible for the members of our community who have developed this expertise through hands-on experience to share their knowledge more widely.

Caring and Responsibility

When I first came to America, I was still thinking in largely traditional terms about appropriate ways to teach and practice the teachings. What I have learned here is the value—as a Dharma practice—of applying the teachings to work toward the goals one holds most dear. I have discovered that it can be deeply inspiring to take advantage of each opportunity that time makes available to us, shaping each moment so that new forms can emerge.

I do not mean to make this process sound automatic or effortless. Not all our projects have been successful, nor have we been able to implement perfectly the teachings that we try to practice. I have undertaken projects in India and Nepal, and also in this country, that ran into serious obstacles, so that in the end we had to turn away with our original plans unrealized. Even in projects that we have completed successfully, we have had to deal with unexpected difficulties that drained our resources and our energy. Persevering in the face of obstacles and disappointments is a vital part of the path, yet it can be disheartening to see the same problems come up again and again.

Everyone in our organization has learned that working for the Dharma is no protection against the standard, frustrating patterns of samsaric mind. Personal likes and dislikes, disagreements and critical judgments, and the dictates of the self-image can undermine every positive effort. Enthusiasm at the start of a project can soon give way to short-sighted and selfish views. We can all be distracted by personalities, fall victim to harmful influences, lose patience when obstacles arise, and choose our own comfort over the effort needed to bring about success.

Often at the beginning of a project I am able to convey something alive and vivid that touches my students and sets the work in motion. But gradually the dynamic begins to fade. Once the energy level on the project drops below a certain point, personal concerns come to the fore. Soon these concerns are driving the momentum of the work in a different direction, or else have slowed it to a near standstill. At this point the inner value and deeper dimensions of the project disappear from view. Individuals begin to insist on their own weakness and limitations, as though it were a point of pride. The work becomes a burden, and I start to hear from every side that what I am asking cannot be done.

Once the project becomes just an ordinary job, the stage is set for a series of painful confrontations. My sense of urgency to complete the project may make little sense to my students, and they may view my wish to create the best possible offering for the Dharma as a series of unreasonable and even arbitrary demands.

To cope with these patterns, I find that I have to clarify again and again the initial inspiration for the project. This is not surprising, for when students have only a limited background, it can be difficult for them to understand the value of what they are doing. Still, it is disheartening to see how the energy of a project slackens when I ask people to work from a Dharma motivation instead of appealing to their personal interests. It is also discouraging to have to counter these tendencies repeatedly and watch as intelligence and enthusiasm give way once again to dullness and resentment. But if these tendencies go unchallenged, these same individuals, preoccupied and distracted by their focus on the self and its galaxy of needs, fall back almost reflexively into the old patterns that have led them to pass through life half asleep.

A focus on self is a part of samsara, characteristic of human beings everywhere. What I have found most difficult in our own work, however, is a characteristic lack of deep caring that seems to spring from the restlessness of the modern mind. It is never easy to apply oneself consistently to work that has value beyond the limited perspective of the self, and this restlessness, which keeps involvement shallow and suspect, makes achievement almost impossible. In this situation, it is not only the work that suffers, but also the individual who wishes to develop emotionally and spiritually. Unless we care deeply and steadily, how can we keep our goal always in mind and pursue the countless details that arise, one after another?

The need for developing a depth of caring that persists through all obstacles is not an easy lesson to learn, and there have been times when my inability to communicate this central truth has left me feeling deeply frustrated. I have seen how difficult it is for even my close students to maintain an unwavering Dharma perspective, the necessary basis for trust between teacher and disciple. This level of trust comes from honesty, honesty from discipline, and discipline from a deep-rooted selfless conviction and commitment. When these qualities waver, it likely that there are hidden problems and that the work is being carelessly done. In these instances, I must play the role of 'boss', which only reinforces the tendency for students to take on the complementary role of 'sullen worker'. The fact that all this is so predictable, so routine for everyone involved, makes it still more painful. In the end the work may get done, but the cost on both sides is high.

Unfortunately, the knowledge that could preserve us from such pain seems to mature only slowly through the years, too late for us to prevent the karma we have brought about from ripening. If my own skills were greater, my ability to deal with and break through these patterns might have developed more rapidly, but this has not happened. And even if other lamas who come after me have greater knowledge and skills, they will almost certainly face the same patterns and the same challenges.

The antidote for what can be heart-wrenching difficulties is for students to develop a solid foundation of faith in the Dharma. When their connection to the teachings and the lineage is firmly rooted in their hearts, they can be clear on their goals, and the rest will come easily. But none of this happens automatically. It takes a long time for students to find the way to make Dharma work their own work, inseparable from their deepest concerns and their path of inner development.

Still, I do see progress. In recent years, as the form of the Nyingma mandala has matured and its symbols have become visible for all to see, students can appreciate more vividly the value of their efforts and accomplishments over the past twenty years or so. More able to draw on the power of the virtuous activity they have embarked upon, they can activate its meaning within their own awareness and sense the blessings that this way of working invites. As they begin to see the connections between the qualities that have developed within them and the Dharma work that they have been doing, the purpose of practicing generosity, discipline, patience, effort, concentration, and wisdom becomes clearer, and they begin to perceive deeper meanings in what they do. These are positive signs that this path can take hold in their hearts, enabling the Dharma to transform their lives and shine through their actions. I can only hope that this momentum will continue to accelerate.

Work as a Path of Learning

My time in the West has been rich with rewards. In particular, I feel tremendous satisfaction when I reflect that the symbols of the Dharma have now found a home in America, that important basic writings have been translated, and that sacred texts and art are being made available to the Tibetan people and preserved for the future.

If I had chosen to stay in India or Nepal after my departure from Tibet, I might have gone on a personal retreat. Perhaps I would have established a center for Dharma study or assisted in founding a monastery. Still, many qualified individuals have undertaken such projects. Here in America, I have been able to make a unique contribution. The availability of modern technology has enabled us to achieve results that would have been unthinkable in Tibet. Even so, without models or precedents to follow, I was constantly challenged to develop new knowledge in order to bring these results into being.

Working in an unfamiliar culture, attempting to explain my vision of what is valuable to students and friends with no previous exposure to Buddhism, has been a remarkable experience. I have had to steadily rethink and reformulate basic concepts and look for new and more effective ways of communicating. I have also had the opportunity to learn countless new skills, from management to finance, and to receive extensive hands-on training in what might be called applied psychology. I have learned how Westerners think, and through them I have learned some very important things about the human condition.

Interacting with my students day after day, focusing on the countless decisions necessary to bring our projects to fruition, I have had no choice but to involve myself totally in activities that I believed had value. Even the frustrations I have lived through have their value, for the teachings of the First and Second Noble Truths—suffering and the origins of suffering—have been very real and present in my own experience.

If none of this has been easy for me, it has certainly not been easy for my students either. I know very well that I am not the only one to lose patience and grow frustrated, nor the only one to feel trapped by patterns of miscommunication. I do not discount the fact that my students have worked for long years on projects whose meaning they have not fully understood, and I am deeply grateful for the confidence they have shown in my vision. My way of showing thanks for all they have done is to give them as many new and challenging jobs as I can, so that they can continue to develop their practice and their understanding.

My students have entrusted their spiritual welfare into my hands. Mindful of this responsibility, I have made a firm commitment not to waste their time. I see it as my duty to educate them in the value and significance of the Dharma, and to assure that their efforts are meritorious. As they master different skills and devote their efforts to a good cause, they also develop the discipline they need to be productive in whatever they do. They learn not to 'space out', not to waste their time in empty or meaningless activity. Their lives become full and rich, reflecting the benefits that flow from their efforts.

The more we can make the value of our work the focus of our awareness, the more we learn. Through the years, the stress and strain of our work has taught us that life is short, and that we must dedicate ourselves to finding meaning in our daily activities. Above all, we have learned that we can do what other people have told us is impossible, that we can break through every limit to arrive at real accomplishment. As these lessons take hold, I sense within our community the growth of a greater awareness and sensitivity, as well as the beginnings of new appreciation and joy.

I cannot say that I have been fully successful in communicating to my students the qualities of caring, love, and appreciation for the tradition, and also for each other, that would assure the transmission forward of the lineage in this new land. Still, there have been significant developments. I hope that in the years to come individuals learn to recognize and weigh carefully the consequences of their attitudes and actions. To my mind, this is the best guarantee of obtaining meaningful results and contributing to the welfare of future generations.

Passing on the Benefits

The training I received in Tibet did not prepare me for many of the duties I have had to take on to make our projects successful. Mostly I have had to devise my own methods of accomplishing our goals, and as a consequence have made many mistakes. But I am not disappointed with the results. If someone had handed me a list in 1969 of everything our organizations would have created by the year 2000, it would have seemed like a wild and impossible dream. Yet today our accomplishments are visible to everyone, and we have done this more or less by ourselves, with little outside support.

Having lived through these experiences myself, I know first-hand the limitations we faced at every level. If we had enough money, we did not have the necessary knowledge or skills; if we had enough knowledge; we did not have the money; if we had both money and knowledge, we did not have enough people; if we had the people, they did not have the patience, discipline, or insight to cope with the new challenges the project presented. On certain projects we were learning a whole new process or skill every few weeks, either learning by doing or trying to take advantage of a few hours of instruction. At every step we made costly mistakes and had to confront our limits and weaknesses. Sometimes it just seemed like pure exhaustion. Over and over I learned the meaning of the American expression, "Two steps forward, one step back."

That is why the results we have achieved strike me as so remarkable. Anyone who has worked to bring even one of these projects into being knows personally how many details and problems come up, how many decisions need to be made. Yet we have had countless such projects, each involving an broad array of details. I may be able to trace how a particular project took form and remember precisely the part that each of us played, but often I find it impossible to connect these efforts with the finished product. Some of our projects are simply too vast to believe we could have actually planned and carried them through to completion.

When I try to make sense of this, I find myself going beyond rational explanations. One way to think about the results of our efforts is to accept that these projects simply needed to happen. If the potential is there and the knowledge available, it is possible for events to explode into time. That seems to be what has occurred here. From a religious perspective, one might speak of prayers being answered; from a Buddhist perspective one might speak of a convergence of karmic circumstances.

In any event, I am certain that what we have accomplished is not my doing. Even if I were much smarter and more clever, even if I had a clear and unerring vision of the future and a careful plan for achieving each aim, I could never have obtained such results based solely on my own desires and will power. My skills, experience, and resources are just too limited, and the pieces of the puzzle are too diverse. Over and over I have had to make decisions without really knowing what was best; time and again I have had to go past the boundaries of my knowledge. When the results have so consistently proved fruitful, what can I do but speak of blessings, or say that time and space and knowledge have come together in mysterious ways?

Perhaps in the end explanations do not matter. My experience convinces me that working in this way, with a steady focus on results, is a path certain to produce satisfaction. Life presents countless opportunities for getting caught up in self-image, political maneuvering, or concern with status. But when we are continually jockeying for position, we can easily miss the chance to accomplish something meaningful with the short time we are given. If we use our time well, staying true to the vision of what we can accomplish for others, we can be confident of making a lasting contribution. Whether we are feeling joy or pain, whether others approve of our work and appreciate our efforts or criticize and complain, what matters is our commitment and clarity, and our confidence in the value of our work.

The Value of Dharma Work

When we work to serve the Dharma, we are adding to a vast treasure house whose wealth will be used to bring benefit to all. At the same time, we are setting an example that others can follow. My students cannot expect much in the way of financial compensation for their long years of effort, but this sense of achievement is one clear reward. I hope that they value it.

Another benefit to our way of working is the progress we have made toward establishing a positive, healthy way of life. Even though we may sometimes face difficult conditions, the underlying tone within our organizations has been positive. We have learned to let go of self-indulgence and keep our focus on achieving what we truly value. We have learned the fleeting nature of social pressures and personal feelings. Certainly, we are sometimes short-sighted and make mistakes; we see later how things could have been done better and get absorbed in the typical dramas, confusions, and emotions. Yet such obstacles tend to play themselves out fairly quickly, and then we go on with the work. This too is a valuable lesson that I hope we can pass on to others.

For such a small community, the range of experience and skills we have is remarkable. Having acquired the knowledge needed for each project as we went along, we are now accomplished in book design and production, in construction, in the creation of various forms of art, in research, writing, and translation, in gilding and etching, in computer technology, in the creation of ritual objects, and in administration of all kinds. We have gained skills in some truly unusual crafts and have engaged in numerous projects that have enabled us to work with precious materials.

The benefits from this way of working are manifold. Some individuals have taken skills they learned here and created successful careers for themselves elsewhere. The rest of us are constantly reaping rewards from the education our work so richly provides, and from the beautiful environment in which we live and work. Most important, the results speak for themselves. We have benefited, America has benefited, and Tibetans have benefited.

The heart of what Buddhism has to offer, passed on by generations of enlightened masters, has no tangible form, and in this sense it is not easily transmitted. Yet the forms our community has created could be seen as a bridge to that inner, invisible level of the teachings. The approach we have evolved is realistic and down to earth. As we create, preserve, and observe, we grow familiar with every aspect of the teachings. As we transmit to others—through texts, through art and ritual, through the opportunity to enter a mandala realm—we are planting a seed that may one day yield rich fruit.

Odiyan: Dharma as a Way of Life

How one fits the Dharma into daily life is largely up to the individual, but external circumstances also play an important role. In this respect, Westerners operate at a disadvantage. Even people who love the Dharma and have deeply meaningful meditation experiences have to find ways to integrate the teachings into a culture that lacks an informed concept of Buddhism. Somehow they have to blend with society—accommodating the expectations of family and friends, the need to earn a living, and much more. It is by no means easy.

Within our community, Odiyan suggests one answer to this dilemma. At Odiyan, the conflict between the demands of daily life and the path of the Dharma largely disappears. Here students can live quite independently, in a positive, healthy environment that is attractive to almost everyone. Free of the need to be concerned about the high cost of living, pollution, commuting, economic downturns, and the like, people at Odiyan can focus on the essentials of Dharma practice. At the same time, the simple, rural lifestyle we have adopted is not that far removed from the mainstream of Western society. When we meet our neighbors, there is a sense that we have much in common, including a deep appreciation for the land on which we live.

Life at Odiyan is rich with beauty and delight. The qualities of silence and sunlight, of wind and rain and growing plants, of Dharma symbols and monuments, can bring joy to the heart. The work itself offers training in discipline, while the setting accommodates inner calm and greater sensitivity to the healing power of nature and the splendor of the Dharma. We have a vast library of traditional texts available for study in the future, and the presence of sacred symbols invites a continuous flow of blessings. Even a single week at Odiyan may reveal the availability of a positive, healing energy and a different kind of knowledge. Such supportive conditions and circumstances are rare in today's world, and I am pleased that we can offer them to sincere and dedicated students.

Of course, not everyone will respond positively to such circumstances all the time. Sometimes it happens that individuals working on a project give up in the middle and leave, or decide that what we have to offer no longer fits with their own personal goals. Some students who stay on, even those who learn to appreciate the lineage of realization and the significance of sacred images and monuments, sometimes complain that there is too much to do, too much responsibility, too little time for personal study and practice. My answer is simple: Whatever has value also has a cost. Only when we learn to implement our values, participate in the tradition, endure and make sacrifices, and be consistent in pursuing our vision will the real meaning of the Dharma become clear.

None of us can always measure up to this standard, but all of us can rediscover again and again the value of hard work and commitment. The sigh that escapes our lips when we prepare to face another job is not just a sign that we are tired: In some ways it is an affirmation. Whoever has sighed in this way knows what I mean. To comprehend the reality that underlies appearances, to perceive the beauty encapsulated in the inspiring image that meets our eyes: That is knowledge well worth having.

The Transforming Wisdom
of the Dharma

*H*aving explored the path to liberation through its progressive stages, the great masters of the Buddhist tradition reported back to us on their discoveries. In their writings, they clarified how the five paths (mārga), the ten stages (bhūmi), the six perfections (pāramitā), and the thirty-seven wings of enlightenment are guideposts along the way, pointers that show us how to proceed step by step, developing our experience progressively. If we treat these teachings with respect and put them into effect, the Dharma becomes a witness to the meaning of enlightenment. Following these pointers, we learn through intimate experience how to overcome each obstacle we encounter. We learn how to manifest a way of being that goes beyond the limits of the human condition.

Like the eighty-four siddhas, each of us must develop our own way of advancing toward enlightenment, in accord with our own mind, our own karma, and the dynamic rhythm of our life. Still, as we extend our awareness and develop skills and powers of discernment, the great masters can be our guides and our witnesses, dispelling confusion, showing us what is genuine, and revealing the next steps along the way. By reflecting on their lives, we can identify what actions we can take, find the inspiration to do more, and affirm the authenticity of experiences that arise. Their example can reveal our potential and their blessings can help us to wake up. The Dharma and those who embody the Dharma appear in the world for just this purpose.

To understand what this means, we need only look at the life of the Buddha. The whole aim of the Buddha's efforts, the entire purpose of his journey toward boundless knowledge, was to lead sentient beings to enlightenment. The scriptures he left behind and the lineage he founded make it possible for us to duplicate his achievement. To follow this path—to gain access to this knowledge and develop conviction in its power—makes our life worthwhile. Nothing on this planet has more value.

Must we accept on faith that this is so? The teachings show otherwise. Instead of fixed dogmas, they offer a path of inquiry, a way for each person to investigate what is true and worthwhile. That is why I have made great efforts to preserve the whole body of texts passed down in the Nyingma lineage. For now, these works exist only in the Tibetan language, but that can change, for the language they speak is universal. For now, they have been brought to fruition only by great masters of the past, but that too can change. Any mind can embody their truth and all experience can manifest their beauty.

Buddhist scriptures offer the transforming power of sacred art, the wisdom of the highest philosophy, the knowledge of a comprehensive cosmology. They offer a vision and a path of meditative realization that allow each person to be his or her own guide. Even though only a handful of the hundred thousand topics that the Buddha taught have been preserved, the texts that survive encompass a wealth of knowledge beyond expressing.

More than twenty-five hundred years ago, the Buddha embraced in his own being complete and total liberation from samsara, and his teachings communicate this experience. Recorded from within samādhi by the enlightened Arhats and Bodhisattvas, who drew on their own transcendent knowledge to pass on a realization identical to that of the Buddha, these teachings are not the product of human interpretation. They express an awareness so far beyond our ordinary mind that we can only call it magical. And yet it is a magic we can embody.

The Dharma reveals how to look at the operation of karma and kleśa and how to investigate the way that samsara is fabricated. It offers the beauty of a cosmos in which every manifestation, including our own mind and emotions, expresses the nature of the Buddha. It presents a path that opens into unimaginable experience.

Miraculously, we are the ones who can follow this path. We are the ladder to realization, the link through which perfect awareness manifests in the world. Our human being is the very core of enlightenment. How do we know this to be so? Because the Buddha himself undertook the great experiment. Manifesting in human form, he dedicated his life to determining whether we human beings could attain realization of the highest truth and liberation from all suffering. Like us, he was born, grew up, played youthful games, received an education, married, and established a family. Like us, he became familiar with the samsaric world and personal concerns. Like great teachers in other traditions, he learned how to attain the highest spiritual levels of being. All this he knew, and all of it he transcended. Investigating thoroughly, questioning everything, he made the leap beyond conceptualization to the inevitability of enlightenment. Displaying the signs and symbols of perfect realization, he heaped bounty upon bounty, until in the end samsara exploded out of existence. And he did this not just for himself, but for beings everywhere. Dedicating the merit of enlightenment itself to all beings—as only a Buddha can do—he established a lineage and path still available to us today.

All human beings long for a few simple things: peace, joy, love, happiness. The Dharma offers these riches, but it also teaches that we can aim higher. Within each of the countless samādhis that the Enlightened Ones enter are hundreds of thousands of different experiences, each one more advanced, more fulfilling, more rich in qualities of beauty, love, joy, and compassion than anything we can presently imagine. Even to look at a single Sūtra, such as the Avataṁsaka, the Śuraṅgama, or the Prajñāpāramitā, will reveal the immanence of such treasures—not because our ordinary minds can think or evoke them (for they cannot)—but because of the grace of the Enlightened Ones and the blessings of the lineage.

We live in a world where time is too short and space too constricted, and where our knowledge is often unable to provide the answers we are searching for. The time has come to change all this. If our patience is too limited to wait many lifetimes for someone to lead us to this promised land, we must resolve to act for ourselves. Fortunately, we have that capacity. It is only a matter of traversing the short distance between not having access to knowledge and having such access—a small step, but a vast transformation. That is what the Dharma offers: the potential for a personal and global renaissance of unimaginable proportions.

The blessings of the Dharma manifest as light, imbued with the magical power to illuminate darkness. By working to embody the Dharma, we can experiment with this remarkable power. We can cultivate knowledge in the laboratory of human life, discovering for ourselves how to activate the process of transformation. We can learn how mind reaches peace, how old patterns are washed away, how deep-rooted hatreds can lose their power, and how enemies become friends.

The more closely we embrace the mind and the heart, the more brightly the light of wisdom and compassion shines, revealing new dimensions of meaning in all we do. From within the darkness of grasping and confusion, goodness begins to sparkle and shine—first a glimmer, then a glow, until we recognize that light is available everywhere, unrestricted and unlimited. This way of working and living makes our human existence rich, virtuous, complete, and fearless. It opens our way of being to the transforming power of bodhicitta.

As soon as bodhicitta begins to rise within us, we realize that we have a great mission, for what we have come to know is something that can and must be shared with others. Though the task appears monumental, we can call upon the blessings of the Bodhisattvas to help us, for the fruit of their realization resonates through all time and space. It is available here and now. The nature of compassion is tireless, and selfess motivation has no bounds or stopping point.

In the light of realization, we see revealed the enlightened family of beings, bestowing their blessings on all. As Padmasambhava himself proclaimed, the Buddhas of the past are standing behind us, the Buddhas of the present are at our side, and the Buddhas of the future draw us forward, toward the right juncture with the path of liberation. Surrounded by light, we step effortlessly onto that path, rejoicing at our good fortune.

The vision of this inconceivable potential has inspired me to preserve the traditions of Tibet and make them available for posterity. My intention is that each of us experience a final release from suffering and pain. My guiding belief is that if the lineage of realization and the models of kāya, vācā, and citta were to disappear from the face of the earth, the loss would be devastating, even for those who have never heard of the Enlightened Lineage.

Inspired by this conviction, certain that all beings can share in enlightenment, my students and I have done all we could for the sake of those to come. May the visible results of this work reveal how knowledge can manifest in the world, allowing the free creativity of the mind to take shape and form.

The Power of Prayer

*A*ccording to our tradition, prayer and meditative practice are the most effective ways to heal the confusion and pain of samsara. Other approaches to relieve suffering and improve our ways of living have limitations that we seem unable to penetrate. Even technology, the proudest accomplishment of recent times, offers no answers to the problems that erupt everywhere, even in the wealthiest of nations.

It is becoming ever more clear that our efforts to eliminate our problems are not working, and may even be increasing our frustration and discontent. Solutions may relieve suffering in one area of our lives while increasing it in others, or raise ethical issues that confuse us as individuals and divide us as societies. In the quest for material well-being, we seem to be separating ourselves from knowledge that supports the human heart and mind. As our understanding of the human spirit weakens and our educational systems focus almost exclusively on the attainment of materialistic goals, we are forgetting our heritage and losing touch with life's value and beauty. Our time is growing shorter and our lives more pressured and automatic. We are becoming more like the machines that we hoped would free us for a happier and more productive life, but which are instead continuing to emmesh us in new and intractible complexities.

To counteract these tendencies, we need to invoke the blessings of the Buddha, Dharma, and Sangha, develop the motivation that empowers meditation, and exercise our spiritual capacities. Prayer directed to the Enlightened Ones turns the minds toward clarity and knowledge; visualization and chanting joins the energy of body and mind to evoke a more comprehensive vision, and meditation generates the energy and will for realization. Symbols bring forth from our consciousness deeper dimensions of meaning, and surrender to a purpose larger than ourselves opens the doorway to wisdom.

When the mind is eased of distractions and worry, it turns naturally toward contemplation. Thoughts filled with light and joy arise in abundance, inspiring us to wish others could share such happiness. From deep within this quiet joy, prayer arises spontaneously; embracing with compassion the ills we perceive around us, it brings forth wishes for peace and harmony, the balance of natural forces, and knowledge to live more wisely in the world. As prayer wells up in our being, it carries our wishes outward, beyond the barriers of self, offering us glimpses of our inherently enlightened nature. Within the mind thus cleansed of self-centered concerns, it plants the seed of bodhicitta, awakening the aspiration to follow the path of the Bodhisattvas.

Our experience today lacks wisdom, and without it our lives lack substance and satisfaction. We need to allow more light into our consciousness, relieve the darkness that confuses our minds, and open our hearts to a broader understanding of what we can contribute. Through prayer we learn how to ask for this knowledge, how to evoke the power of the lineage that can cut through the darkest obscurations. We come to understand that we can awaken the potential for Buddha-wisdom, develop it through practice, evoke its power through accomplishment, and obtain the results, the blessings for self and others that fill our lives with meaning and abiding joy.

Events of our times indicate that we have entered the kaliyuga, the age of darkness foretold by the Buddha, when confusion and apathy would increase and cloud the Dharma from the eyes of living beings. During this age, frustration and anger increase, poisoning our happiness, sowing the seeds of aggression, greed, and distrust, and fostering loneliness and separation. Shortages manifest in all areas of our lives, yet desires continue to expand, generating more needs, more discord, and more dissatisfaction. The lives of individuals and the course of nations become more confused and chaotic. Caught in the vortex of increasing darkness, we need the best friends we can find: We need the wisdom of Mañjuśrī, the compassion of Avalokiteśvara, the loving-kindness of Maitreya, and the power of Guru Rinpoche, Padmasambhava.

The power of prayer can transform and revitalize the very chemistry of our bodies. It can open our hearts to an inexhausible flow of joy and meaning and our minds to the guidance of the great Bodhisattvas, the best of spiritual friends. We can live, work, and practice with clarity and peace of mind, while developing the six great perfections: giving, morality, patience, effort, meditation, and wisdom.

Guru Padmasambhava said "If you are willing to open your heart, I will help you." Prayer is the path that enables us to respond to this compassionate offer. Visualizing Padmasambhava and the great Bodhisattvas, focusing on their images, and concentrating on our deepest needs, we can bring forth our energy, activate a flow of blessings, and obtain knowledge we can use to restore harmony and balance to our lives. Then we can perceive more clearly what knowledge we are missing, and we can make the effort necessary to bring it into being.

Prayer to the Enlightened Ones

Inspired by the Ceremony for World Peace, 1994

Homage to the Buddhas,
Bodhisattvas, and Great Arhats.

On this sacred ground, World-Honored One, you parted the veils of illusion and demonstrated the most perfect enlightenment. Although thousands of years have passed, the beauty of your knowledge lives on in the Sangha, and its power radiates from this holy place. We sense the presence of your great compassion: it touches our hearts and fills our eyes with tears.

Yet we are far removed from your knowledge, and there is little we really understand. Beings everywhere struggle in darkness. In our frustration we turn against each other; in our hunger we devastate the earth. Our tears could fill oceans, but still we continue to inflict suffering on ourselves and others.

Most supremely Enlightened One, can you teach us in these dark times, when we see the despair that envelopes us but do not know how to end it? Can you guide us now, when realized masters of your lineage, once as numerous as stars in the sky, have passed away, and few are left to train us?

Teach us in these dark times, when faith is diffi-cult to sustain and doubts undermine our confidence and trust. Teach us to pray, that we might be blessed by your compassion and learn how to benefit from your infinite wisdom.

Teach us in these dark times, when we have choices but cannot distinguish what is helpful from what will destroy us; when all our freedoms do not relieve our minds of worry, our bodies from stress, our hearts from the torment of the emotions.

Teach us in these dark times, when problems beset us on every side, when illness invades us without our knowing, when we have no place to go and no idea of where we are going. Open our hearts to understanding when the results of our actions come back to us; bestow your compassion when we see too late the pain we have caused and the damage to our world we could have prevented.

Teach us the consequences of self-centered views and selfish actions that starve us of the blessings of love and devotion. Teach us in our time of need, as we grow older and loved ones leave us, when the bodies we tended so carefully become a burden in our old age and our memories a source of pain. Help us to see how to care for ourselves and turn our minds toward beauty. Fill our eyes with images of enlightened being, our hearts with the joy of meaning, and our bodies with the bliss of lasting satisfaction.

While we thirst for fulfillment, our minds are swayed by desire and entranced by the dancing flow of emotions. Rushing after pleasures, chasing visions of delight, chased in turn by anxiety and fear, we rarely touch the inner silence that heals and restores. We yearn for happiness as one lost in a desert yearns for water, but we do not know where to find it. Too late we realize we have pursued the shifting visions of mirage. Exhausted, we hear the echo of Mara's mocking voice and glimpse the insight that impelled you toward the Bodhi Tree and the Seat of Enlightenment.

Without your guidance, what fears will fill our hearts in our declining years? On whom can we rely for protection? Our societies are not enlightened; our leaders make mistakes, and we cannot always trust their direction.

In the entire world there is only one supremely realized Buddha. Only you have penetrated the net of illusion and manifested the fullest meaning of human life, only you can bring forth the light of knowledge and dispel the darkness of our time.

The walls around us are thick and strongly built; we can hardly feel your compassion. Our understanding is clouded by self-deceptions, and our faith is weak. Our view is too limited to comprehend the vastness of your vision.

Can we take refuge in you, most blessed one? Can you share with us as you shared with masters in the past the knowledge you received here on the Diamond Throne? We need your blessing to break the chains of karma, stronger than tempered steel, heavy with the weight of repeated error. We need your inspiration to develop a more expansive consciousness and a more penetrating virtue. We need your blessing to cultivate a mind that thirsts to realize enlightened knowledge and a heart open enough to receive it.

Heal our hearts with the beauty of śīla, which grows from the practice of Vinaya; heal our bodies with the elixir of samādhi and our minds with the liberating realization of prajñā. Share with us your compassion and your wisdom, so we can develop your matchless qualities and become part of you.

Following in your footsteps, we can close off the endless flow of desires and free ourselves of guilt, weakness, and fear. With heart, mind, and senses attuned to your message, we can bring forth all our resources for knowledge and realize the unlimited potential of human consciousness.

May we become like you, able to offer body, speech, and mind for the benefit of all beings. Most beautiful Enlightened One, guide us that we may merge with your path.

PART TWO

Conversations
with Tarthang Tulku

Knowledge of the mandala has its origins in the enlightenment of the Buddha Śākyamuni. As the Blessed One demonstrated for the benefit of all beings, when the obscurations to realization drop away, all forms can be seen as emerging from space in a process of continual becoming. From within this wider perspective, everything the human mind names and establishes as fixed is subject to change, and any thought and experience can be shaped into forms that direct the mind toward enlightenment. This realized truth is encoded in the structure of the mandala.

Working Within the Mandala

Rinpoche, you do not seem to teach in the traditional way. How are you actually teaching your students?

A starting point is for people to see their weakness—this is the basis for building strength. Another aspect is to introduce certain kinds of experience through meditation or analysis that can be valuable in opening the mind. This may seem different from the traditional teachings, but I would say that what we do here does not depart from the tradition.

The Nyingma path is based on the teaching that the work we do is inseparable from the Dharma. This is easy enough to say, but it can be hard to put into effect. It means that if we value the Dharma, we must value our work. If we honor the Dharma, we must honor our work. To integrate Dharma and work so that our work becomes our very heart and soul—this is the path that makes each individual into an integral part of the Sangha.

In this country, the spiritual path is often viewed as a form of escape from responsibility and the realities of daily life. But the distinction between the worldly and the spiritual is imposed from the view of worldliness, not from within the spiritual tradition. In Buddhism, the foundation of practice is the intention to benefit others, and this naturally means playing an active role in the world. This is especially true in contemporary life, where virtually every aspect of life is entangled in worldly concerns.

Traditionally, Buddhists cultivate the inner value and meaning of life through meditation, prayer, and devotion. But the attitudes that underlie such conduct can also be expressed in work, so that work itself becomes meditation and prayer. The common factor that creates the link is the compassion that we feel for the suffering of others, coupled with the sincere intention to act for their benefit.

Recognizing the importance of our work does not mean that work should be taken on as a duty alone. That attitude can turn even simple tasks into unpleasant chores. Instead, we can allow our love and our compassion to feed the joy that we naturally feel when we use our capacities to the fullest.

There is a special honesty in giving our fullest effort that renews and revitalizes us. When we work in this way, the energy behind our work can flow free of restriction. Our energy can build on itself, generating rhythm and momentum. Just as a broad and powerful river shapes its own course and creates its distinctive landscape, the efforts powered by this free-flowing energy can produce unique and distinctive results. This dynamic is inherently joyful—it carries us beyond the reach of anxiety and heightens our will to push through obstacles. A sense of joy in our work is a valuable sign that our actions have true value. When we truly cherish what we are doing, our actions take on a special power, and their positive influence unfolds in unforeseen directions. We can work long hours without feeling the exhaustion that comes from conflict, emotional turmoil, and resistance. We work lightly and easily, and still we accomplish a great deal. We work quickly, but we do not tire.

What insights inspired you to develop your emphasis on work as a form of teaching?

Work is creativity. I have found from my own experience that actively engaging in shaping our own lives is deeply stimulating. At the same time, work is a way to preserve the Dharma and the lineage in response to present conditions, and to make a contribution to our fellow beings.

Since we inhabit this world, we must find a way to work within it. We ourselves may not be materialistic, but we must learn to work with the materialistic dimension. On the simplest level, we must first guarantee our survival. Then we need the resources that will enable us to accomplish what is positive. Manifesting knowledge within the world, we demonstrate the unfailing quality of the Dharma.

Being Dharma students means we can be at least as successful as others, perhaps even much more successful. The worldly knowledge we acquire can be turned to higher purposes, while our work in the world can become a challenge that awakens and refines higher knowledge.

What do you view as the main factors in success, and how do these factors relate to a religious way of life?

Our human embodiment supplies us with everything we need for success, but people often misuse their abilities. If people lack integrity, even the best goals and visions cannot come into being. If the producer is not reliable, the product will not be reliable, no matter how fine the natural material is. The best resources and most stable funding will not lead to success without willingness to take responsibility and the determination to succeed. If we look on the immediate individual level, we can see these shortages displayed before us every day. They manifest in our being easily distracted or sidetracked from one task to another. And they show up as holes in the fabric of our work patterns.

Responsibility, integrity, and determination all depend on our level of awareness, concentration, and energy. These fundamental human resources provide the foundation for developing positive qualities and creative activity, and we can begin right now to refine them. Without pressuring or forcing ourselves, we can gently exercise our concentration to develop a light but steady focus. As concentration grows stronger, awareness is not so readily lost. We stay more closely connected to our experience.

It is this connectedness and intelligence that brings genuine quality and reliability to our work. When we have the tools and the materials we need, and we are in full accord with the guiding vision, we can develop the 'feel' of what we are doing. Each type of work has a texture and rhythm, a shape and form we can relate to. When we are tuned in to these inner aspects of work, we know what we are doing in a direct and immediate way. Awareness opens up, concentration holds the direction steady, and energy flows smoothly. We begin to enjoy a creative exchange with the world that feeds back to us and further stabilizes and deepens our effort.

Without a steady focus, awareness will not develop; without strong energy, concentration does not cohere; without awareness, concentration and energy are misdirected. The ancient technique of contemplation brings concentration, awareness, and energy into harmony. It refines these integral aspects of human being simultaneously. By working at this ground level, we build integrity and determination, and we develop the capacity to take full responsibility for our lives.

Through the ages, awareness, concentration, and energy have always played the central role in spiritual development. If we do not exercise and develop these resources, they begin to weaken. As their power diminishes, we lose the ethical impulses and the spiritual potential that are the crowning glory of human life. Life grows more mechanical, artificial, and automatic. Eventually we begin to rely ever more strongly on technology to provide solutions to problems that human intelligence can no longer offer. At this point, humanity faces great dangers.

If our community can demonstrate how to increase awareness, concentration, and energy and forge them into tools for improving responsibility, integrity, and determination, we will be able to benefit society through our example. Knowledge of how to change negative patterning is the most precious gift we could offer. If we educate ourselves, testing our knowledge, refining it, and manifesting it in our accomplishments, we will be able to make a lasting difference in the world.

Many religious traditions make a strong distinction between worldly and spiritual concerns. Are you suggesting that these distinctions are less important in modern life?

The separation between spiritual and worldly ways of life has long gone unquestioned, but in today's world, such a division is simply no longer workable. The strict hierarchies and shared beliefs that supported it in the past are vanishing. Spiritual communities and individuals cannot afford to leave worldly affairs to others, for they can no longer count on support from the larger society. Nor do most individuals following secular pursuits draw sustenance from the efforts of those who attend to the concerns of the spirit. What made this distinction between worldly and spiritual paths work was a sense of a deep underlying connection between the spiritual and the worldly realms. Today, that connection seems to be disappearing.

Based on my experience since coming to the West more than thirty years ago, I am convinced that this split between the world of work and the concerns of the spirit is not necessary. Work itself can have inner meaning and value that make it part of the spiritual path. Anyone who does any kind of work can taste the sense of deep inner fulfillment that has always been considered the fruit of a spiritual way of living, even if he or she feels no sense of religious vocation.

What do you consider the most valuable aspects of work as a spiritual practice?

The focus on work lets individuals apply the living Dharma to their daily lives instead of treating it as a matter of theory. Work can be a form of study, while at the same time it produces tangible results. For example, the six perfections have a place in all our activities. Undertaken with an attitude of serving others, our work is a form of giving. When I write books, I am studying what I write; when I work patiently, I am meditating on patience. The same is true for concentration, vigor, and discipline.

When work is also practice, both sides reinforce each other. We become more productive, and from time to time we can catch a glimpse of our full potential as human beings. There is also the satisfaction of

having accomplished something of value to ourselves and possibly to others.

Nyingma students benefit from work in many
ways. Learning to work is an antidote to laziness. In
our community, the traditional forms we work with
awaken the mind to new knowledge, which leads
toward growth and understanding. Work is a form
of karma yoga: It generates merit and shapes the
foundation for the path.

Work is also the most direct way of dealing with
some typical obstacles that Western students have
to confront. Some people may seek out the spiritual
way of life because they think it will let them escape
the ordinary world—a kind of early retirement.
Work shows them the need for engaging the world
honestly and directly, which accords with the purpose of spiritual practice. Sometimes people think
that because they are 'spiritual', they are above dealing with mundane concerns, but such a fixed, rigid
position can undermine inspiration. Dharma work
helps them become more flexible and creative.

We could say that work is a preparation for
higher practices, but this is only one way of viewing
the value of work in a spiritual path. As the lives of
the eighty-four siddhas show, work can serve a
more important and immediate purpose. We can
live the highest goal *within* ordinary work activities.
With this orientation, the *path* of preparation can
also become the *fruit* of preparation.

Nyingma students appear to find their path a difficult one. Are these difficulties real, or are they self-created?

The Nyingma teachings may involve physical and mental effort, but they are not inherently difficult. There are no secret teachings or initiations that impose strenuous requirements. We emphasize preliminary practices that are safe but also beneficial.

Some individuals may view this way of teaching as difficult because it does not promise quick answers or magic solutions. But the way of life we encourage is stable and grounded, so there is a foundation for dealing with problems. Older students gradually develop a fuller understanding of the teachings and become more aware of the consequences of their actions. Then their lives become more simple and their path easier to conduct.

The real difficulty seems to come for people who do not have this kind of grounding and find themselves blown back and forth by every emotional wind. When the force of the wind picks up, students who have not established a firm foundation for their practice may experience very serious difficulties. That much is true.

Is this practice particularly suited to the West?

Westerners have a practical quality that makes work very suitable as their Dharma practice. When they apply themselves to work, they can see clearly what they have accomplished. Of course, the West is technologically advanced, so that is another advantage. Effort put into work here can produce more significant results than the same effort could produce elsewhere. Also, at this early stage in the transmission of the Dharma, work may have an advantage over meditation alone because it has a definite impact on one's life and consciousness. Someone may sit in meditation for ten years, chanting and carrying out other practices, but if there is a lack of preparation, concentration, and vision, the result may be limited. If this is so, there can be deep disappointment, a sense that all that time has been wasted. But if that time is spent in productive work, there are tangible results that can be a source of encouragement and satisfaction. And the work itself can provide rich and rewarding experiences.

It is true that time flies and that opportunities disappear before we recognize them for what they are. And it is true as well that time can pass slowly, presenting one task after another and promising nothing but tedium and exhaustion. Yet beneath such surface manifestations, time operates differently. In the deeper currents of time, merit projects itself forward, and actions link up to a deeper, more meaningful dynamic. Once we touch this level, feelings of enjoyment or exhaustion, or of being overwhelmed by difficulties, seem less significant.

The issue is actually very simple. If the merit of your efforts outlives the energy you give, the price is not too high to pay. Looking at my own work and the work of those in our community, I hope and believe that this is the case. I am confident that our creations have real value, for humanity now and for future generations.

Over the past thirty years we have made thousands of prayer wheels and prayer flags, built the Odiyan Stupa and temples, and created hundreds of statues and other works of sacred art. Through intensive publishing projects, we have preserved more than a thousand paintings, each an artistic masterpiece, as well as thousands of volumes of valuable texts. I firmly believe that the texts we have preserved and the symbols we have created will bring great benefit to the West, no matter what the outcome of our other efforts.

Are your students developing the qualifications to pass on the Nyingma lineage?

The Nyingma teachings are extensive, a veritable ocean of Dharma. There are the bKa'-ma teachings of Mahā, Anu, and Ati Yoga, and the gTer-ma teachings transmitted by Padmasambhava and other great masters at the time of Khri-srong lDe'u-btsan, which were recovered at a later time. I have not tried to transmit these directly. Until now I have focused on presenting basic Dharma teachings in order to establish a good foundation. There has been a slow, steady growth, and I feel that in time, there may be opportunities for additional teachings to come out. Whether this happens or not depends on my students.

The scope of Buddhism is very vast. It is not surprising that it can take years of sustained effort for students to develop a genuine understanding of the teachings and appreciation for their value to their lives. Although we have put a priority on building a foundation for the Dharma rather than on traditional practice and study, I encourage students to spend time each day in meditation and to read our publications, including the volumes in the Crystal Mirror series, which introduce the history, philosophy, and practices of the Dharma and the Nyingma tradition. Students work with these teachings continually while editing and preparing our books for publication. Many members of our community— even those with no artistic training—have had valuable opportunities to understand the connection between aesthetic appreciation and spiritual practice by working with many different forms of sacred art and helping to build our temples. Our long-term students have also traveled to India and Nepal to participate in the World Peace Ceremonies at Bodh Gaya, Sarnath, and Kathmandu. This contact with traditional practice, especially in these holy places, is important to their understanding of the lineage and the nature of the spiritual path. All these activities are forms of education that penetrate deeply.

Since the work of establishing the teachings in Western cultures in a direct and tangible way will have to be taken up by the people of those lands, I have worked to develop their understanding on the deepest level possible. In the process, students are making a good contribution to the Dharma, which is auspicious for the future of Buddhism in America.

Based on your experience, what do you think will be the future of Buddhism in the West?

If no direct obstacles arise, I believe that a Sangha can be established in the West. It may not be a Sangha that follows the Tibetan tradition or any other tradition; instead, it may create its own tradition and its own way of communicating the Dharma. For this to happen in a way that preserves the beauty and transformative power of the Dharma, there must be a solid foundation. This is what we have been working to set in place. It may take more years of effort before we can be satisfied that the foundation has been fully prepared, but I think that the reward will be worth the price.

Living Within the Mandala

Rinpoche, you describe Odiyan as a mandala, but most people think of mandalas as patterns painted in thankas or defined in colored sand. Are mandalas truly three-dimensional, or is Odiyan unique in this respect?

The mandala serves as a pattern that structures the energy of enlightenment into forms that the human senses can perceive. These forms are symbols that connect the structures of the mind with the activity of the Enlightened Ones. They empower realization and give the meditator access to universal reality.

Although the concept of mandala has no equivalent in the Western view of reality, it is central to the Mantrayāna view and practice. Many hundreds of mandalas exist to serve specific needs of different individuals, and each mandala promotes certain kinds of understanding. All schools of Tibetan Buddhism use mandalas in their practice. And yes, mandalas can indeed be represented in three-dimensional forms.

What inspired you to create Odiyan as a mandala, not only in the forms and arrangements of its buildings, but also in its landscaping and gardens?

When I was very young, I would watch as my father prepared for the fire ceremonies that were part of the Heruka sādhanas. After he collected and assembled the materials to be burned, he would build a sand mandala on top of the pile. First he would mark out the size and proportions of the mandala, then he would create the forms in five colors: blue (or white) in the east, yellow in the south, red in the west, green in the north, and white (or blue) in the center. These forms were slightly built up, in relief. That was my earliest understanding of the mandala's forms.

After I began my studies, I read that the structure and meaning of the mandala draw on ancient knowledge of universal correspondences, and that mandalas integrate shapes and colors with the elements and the points of the compass. These forms are symmetrically arranged to represent balance and harmony in the cosmos, in the physical environment, and also in the human mind. I learned how the five Dhyāni Buddhas are associated with the directions of the mandala, and about the peaceful and wrathful deities that could inhabit the mandala forms.

As I began to appreciate the intricate symbolism expressed in each of the mandala's elements, I realized that it was possible to enter the mandala experientially, a meditative practice that corresponds to entering a temple. Later, during my travels through Tibet, I saw a few three-dimensional models of mandalas, the largest being about two feet in diameter. These models reinforced my impression that a mandala, if built on a larger scale, could be inhabited physically. Once this impression took hold, it continued to develop into a rich source of inspiration. When I came to America, the mandala, with its sacred architecture and mutually supportive parts, became the model for the Nyingma organizations in California and in our centers abroad. When we acquired land for our country center in 1975, the idea of creating Odiyan as a mandala arose almost of its own accord.

What would be the purpose and value of living within a mandala, physically or symbolically?

The Mantrayana traditions of Tibet view the mandala as a cosmos, a perfect Buddhafield. In the Sukhāvativyūha and other Mahāyāna Sūtras, Buddhafields are known as pure lands: heaven realms where every form satisfies the senses at the deepest level, and conditions are ideal for attaining enlightenment.

In the mandala of a Buddhafield, the rustle of leaves becomes the sound of voices teaching the Dharma, merging with the tinkle of bells and the subtle rhythms and tones of celestial music. Suffering and death are unknown, all worldly concerns disappear, and joy becomes the natural state of being. Food and drink, all freely available, are transmuted into the rarest of nectars. Those fortunate enough to enter such a pure realm find joy and love welling up within the heart, sustained by sights, sounds, smells, tastes, and sensations conveyed by senses perfectly attuned to beauty. Mind moves effortlessly into meditative awareness, and enlightenment unfolds spontaneously.

All this is on the outer level of meaning and significance. Inwardly, as the texts of the Mantrayāna explain, the term mandala refers to the enlightened field that radiates outward from its own perfect center, much as electrons in an atom arrange themselves around a central nucleus. All points of the mandala are linked to the central point, expressing its dynamic in a ceaseless display of unfolding beauty that conveys the most profound wisdom. As the perfect field of realization, the mandala arrives at no final point that can be touched. It has no root that can be unearthed, and it displays no edge whose location can be discovered.

What exactly does this vision of mandala signify to us as ordinary beings and practitioners?

All beings participate in the body, speech, and mind of the Buddhas and share the potential to become enlightened. The temple, the mandala, and all its realms and symbols heighten awareness of that potential and stimulate us to activate it through our practice. When we live within the mandala, all these processes unfold naturally, until all positive qualities are magnified and all negative ones transformed. At the outset, we may respond only subliminally to Dharma symbols that awaken us to the beauty and truth of enlightened knowledge, but as awareness develops, we begin to perceive our kinship with the Buddhas more clearly and appreciate the unlimited creativity and freedom the mandala offers. Like mind, the mandala allows for infinite manifestations, while remaining completely open and unclaimed. There is nothing in it of substance, nothing that can be traced or defined. As beings bound to particular forms and formulations, we cannot conceive of that unlimited and ultimate aspect of reality, yet the mandala is still available.

Rinpoche, you seem to be speaking of living in the mandala on two levels at once: physically and symbolically. Is it possible to merge these realms? Is this the guiding vision of Odiyan?

As a young man, I found descriptions of the symbolism of the mandala deeply meaningful. Through hearing about enlightened masters and reading their biographies, I sensed that Padmasambhava, Sarahapa, Nāgārjuna, and other great siddhas were able to live fully in the awareness of the realization that the mandala and its symbols express. From their writings and their actions, it is clear that these masters were able to move move back and forth at will from the realm of the mandala to the realm of conventional form. In doing this, they demonstrated that the distance between samsara and the enlightened realm is not as vast as we think, and that we can create and live in a mandala in this time and place.

Knowledge of the mandala's power to awaken the full power of human consciousness was passed on in the texts of the Inner Tantras, many of which were first transmitted in the ancient land of

Oḍḍiyāna. This knowledge inspired the creation of bSam-yas, Tibet's first monastery. It has continued to emerge within the Nyingma teachings ever since.

How can practitioners enter the mandala on this symbolic, experiential level?

We gain entrance to the mandala through devotion to the Buddha, Dharma, and Sangha and appreciation for the opportunity a human life offers to study and practice the teachings of enlightenment. Devotion and appreciation melt the barriers imposed by ego and emotions, revealing gateways to an new realm of beauty and meaning. Within this realm, temples, symbols, and sacred forms manifest spiritual qualities important for us to recognize and meditate upon. For example, the Buddha's form embodies eighty qualities related to enlightenment, and the shape of the stupa calls to mind such teachings as the thirty-seven wings of enlightenment and the stages of the Bodhisattva path.

Appreciation and devotion can initiate a powerful process of transformation. The first step involves a willingness to look directly at the workings of samsara and analyze the nature of mind and emotions. From this foundation, devotion, visualization, and ritual open pathways to direct contact with the Buddha, Dharma, and Sangha. A momentum develops that can transcend all forms of duality. Temple, altar, and sacred images open the closed doors of consciousness, giving access to the relief of confession, the inner strength of morality, and the blessings of communion with the enlightened ones. Through heartfelt surrender we come to appreciate the full significance of the Buddha; we identify with his qualities and can work to perfect them within ourselves.

When we imprint the Four Noble Truths and the Eightfold Path upon our minds, we begin to establish the basis for freeing ourselves from the grasp of karmic obscurations. However selfishly we may begin, the Eightfold Path leads in the right direction, moving unerringly toward wisdom and compassion. Right view brings clarity and focus. Right intention manifests in right speech and in right action that communicates the qualities of the Dharma; it frees us from the causes of guilt and regret, and enables us to be genuinely helpful to others. Right livelihood helps us refrain from actions that cause harm; in its highest expression, it provides opportunities to benefit others. Right efforts bring joy; joy inspires us to apply ourselves willingly to all we do and develop right mindfulness, the alert, wakeful attitude that lets us perceive the truth of the teachings in whatever form they manifest. Right mindfulness strengthens right concentration, the meditation that removes obscurations and illuminates the path to enlightenment.

The Bodhisattva carries this practice further. By taking refuge, the Bodhisattva prays to embody the Buddha's knowledge for the purpose of liberating all sentient beings from the cycles of cause and effect that lead to suffering. The universal scope of this devotion completely extinguishes thought of self and brings the Bodhisattva into deep communion with the Buddha's wisdom.

Symbols and images of realization bring the qualities of enlightenment into our lives at whatever level we are prepared to receive them. When we meditate on images of Buddhas and Bodhisattvas and invoke their qualities through prayer, we step out of the fantasy realm of self-preoccupation and touch the enlightened qualities latent within our being. These qualities develop as our practice matures, removing obscurations and leading us closer to enlightenment. Even if some practitioners initially focus on the image as an entity separate from themselves, this too has benefit, for the qualities they are invoking are pure and perfected. As if seen in a mirror, the qualities awakened through prayer will reflect back to the minds of the worshippers, and their own devotion will activate a process of transformation.

Once we become attuned to their purpose, the symbols and forms of the mandala remind us to reexamine our practice and put forth greater effort to perfect it. Eventually, it is possible to live completely within this experience. All aspects of daily life take on the nature of practice, and the whole of existence manifests as part of the mandala. Each aspect of the mandala is steadily pointing to that level of realization.

Index

Further Readings

Introductions to Buddhism

Ways of Enlightenment: Buddhist Studies at the Nyingma Institute. A non-sectarian guide to the Buddha's essential teachings, based on Lama Mipham's Gateway to Expertise. Prepared under the guidance of Tarthang Tulku.

Footsteps on the Diamond Path, Crystal Mirror 1-3, introduces the Vajrayana through essays on the Nyingma lineage, translation of 14 short works by the Nyingma masters Longchenpa, Lama Mipham, and Paltrul Rinpoche, and essays by Tarthang Tulku.

The Three Jewels and Dharma Transmission, Crystal Mirror 6, offers a traditional presentation of the meaning of Buddha, Dharma, and Sangha. Includes 238 biographies illustrated with line drawings of Indian and Tibetan masters important in the major Dharma lineages.

Light of Liberation, Crystal Mirror 8. A clearly written history of Buddhism in India based on traditional sources, archaeological surveys, and modern histories, with 38 historical maps, charts, and bibliography.

Holy Places of the Buddha, Crystal Mirror 9. An illustrated presentation of the eight traditional holy places, with descriptions of Dharma centers of ancient India and Afghanistan from the journals of Chinese pilgrims and information from archaeological reports.

Masters of the Nyingma Lineage, Crystal Mirror 11. Biographical sketches of more than 350 masters of the Nyingma tradition of Tibetan Buddhism, beginning with teachers active in the time of the Buddha and including the great gTer-stons in all Tibetan traditions.

All books on this page produced by Dharma Publishing.

Translations of Traditional Texts

Buddha

Dhammapada: Essential Teachings of Śākyamuni Buddha. An ancient compilation of four hundred verses on twenty-six topics central to all Buddhist traditions. Translated from a modern Tibetan edition of the original Pali text.

The Voice of the Buddha: The Lalitavistara Sutra. A poetical account of the Buddha's life, enlightenment, and first teachings, illustrated with thankas of the Buddha surrounded by scenes from his life.

Abhidharma

The Arthaviniścaya Sūtra and Its Commentary, a compendium of Abhidharma, translated by N. H. Samtani. A virtual encyclopedia of key terms for Dharma practitioners, with extensive notes and glossary.

Calm and Clear, by Lama Mipham, translated, with commentary by Tarthang Tulku. Clear guides to traditional śamathā and vipaśyana meditation practices by a renowned 18th-century Nyingma master.

Mind in Buddhist Psychology, Yeshe Gyaltsen's Necklace of Clear Understanding, translated by H. V. Guenther and L. S. Kawamura. An analysis of fifty-one basic mental events, with instructions on how to recognize and transform patterns that perpetuate suffering.

Madhyamaka

Master of Wisdom: Six texts by Nāgārjuna, translated by Christian Lindtner. Treatises on śūnyatā, the interconnection of analysis, meditation, and moral conduct, and two works on the qualities of the Buddha.

All books on this page produced by Dharma Publishing.

Books on Dharma Work
as a Spiritual Practice

Skillful Means: Patterns for Success, by Tarthang Tulku. Teachings on the attitudes and actions that ensure success both in work and on the spiritual path, with 24 exercises for developing skills essential for success in both arenas of accomplishment.

Mastering Successful Work: Skillful Means Wake Up! by Tarthang Tulku. Clear and powerful guidance on how to make work into a path of transformation and dynamic accomplishment. With 80 exercises.

Teachings from the Heart, by Tarthang Tulku. Thirty-three essays drawn from book introductions, interviews, and previously unpublished articles introduce central elements of the Buddhist path and suggestions for transforming work into a means of realization.

Ways of Work: Dynamic Action, An overview of the creation of the Nyingma organizations in America, as seen through experiences of Western students interwoven with excerpts from Tarthang Tulku's talks and memos.

Master Work, by Arnaud Maitland. An account of the application and results of an experiment based on the Skillful Means management training system developed by Tarthang Tulku, with exercises designed to help readers transform work into spiritual practice.

All books on this page are produced by Dharma Publishing, a non-profit publisher of Buddhist books and art. Contributions and sponsorship of new books support the publication of teachings and information important to our times. All contributions are tax-deductible.

More books on the web: www.dharmapublishing.com